REAL CHARACTERS

How God uses unlikely people to accomplish great things

REAL CHARACTERS

J. Vernon McGee

THOMAS NELSON PUBLISHERS
Nashville • Atlanta • London • Vancouver

Published in Nashville, Tennessee, by Thomas Nelson, Inc., Publishers, and distributed in Canada by Word Communications, Ltd., Richmond, British Columbia, and in the United Kingdom by Word (UK), Ltd., Milton Keynes, England.

Scripture quotations are from the NEW KING JAMES VERSION of the Bible. Copyright © 1979, 1980, 1982, Thomas Nelson, Inc., Publishers.

ISBN 0-7852-7732-3

Printed in the United States of America

CONTENTS

NEW TESTAMENT

INTRODUCTION

J. Vernon McGee loved the Word of God. And the characters who walked across its pages were not only real people but old friends to him.

Recognizing that God had used them to be examples to us, he studied them carefully. Much of his understanding of the works and ways of God came through his close association with them.

In over fifty years of teaching through the Bible from cover to cover, J. Vernon McGee met all the Bible characters and made them live by stepping into their sandals and reliving their experiences with God, especially little-known folk whom the world has forgotten but God has immortalized.

We trust that you will enjoy meeting some of these folk on the pages of this book which we have compiled from the cassettes of Vernon McGee's tape-recorded messages. And above all else, we pray that your own life will be enriched through your encounter with these *Real Characters*.

Trude Cutler, Editor
Thru the Bible Radio Network

— 1 —

JACOB

Back to Bethel

Then God said to Jacob, "Arise, go up to Bethel and dwell there; and make an altar there to God, who appeared to you when you fled from the face of Esau your brother." And Jacob said to his household and to all who were with him, "Put away the foreign gods that are among you, purify yourselves, and change your garments. Then let us arise and go up to Bethel; and I will make an altar there to God, who answered me in the day of my distress and has been with me in the way which I have gone."
(Genesis 35:1–3)

Bethel is about twelve miles north of Jerusalem. Described as a bleak moorland in the hill country, it stands twelve hundred feet above sea level where the wild winds whistle about its large, exposed rocks. If you have driven over the narrow old roads between California's Yucca Valley and Apple Valley, you have seen a place much like Bethel. Although the topography was desolate and forbidding, it was where the spiritual high point in the life of Jacob occurred.

To understand this passage in Genesis 35, we must go back thirty years to the time when Jacob first went to Bethel. At that time he was fleeing for his life. His brother Esau was after him to murder him. Jacob was a fugitive, a runaway. He had no traveling gear whatsoever except the staff in his hand.

That first night away from home Jacob spent at Bethel, his head pillowed on a stone in that bleak, lonely spot, with the winds howling about him. He dreamed of a ladder that was set up on earth, the top of it reaching to heaven, and God standing above the ladder.

What was it that brought him to this place? What kind of a home did he leave? It was not an ideal home, but it was a home through which God was moving for time and for eternity. It was the home of Isaac and Rebekah.

HOME AND FAMILY

Isaac was the son of Abraham and Sarah, the son of promise God had given them by a miracle in their old age. When the boy was grown, his aged father refused to take a wife for him from among the heathen in whose land they lived. Abraham instructed his servant to get a bride for his son from among his kinfolk back at Haran. The servant, unerringly guided by God, brought back Rebekah to be the bride of Isaac. We take up the thread of their story when they were expecting their first child:

> **But the children struggled together within her; and she said, "If all is well, why am I like this?" So she went to inquire of the LORD. And the LORD said to her:**
>
> **"Two nations are in your womb,**
> **Two peoples shall be separated from your body;**
> **One people shall be stronger than the other,**
> **And the older shall serve the younger."**
> (Genesis 25:22, 23)

God said that two nations were to come out of this family, and two nations did come from these two boys. We shall follow them through the Word of God.

Not only can we trace the history of these two nations, but we are given the spiritual application to the life of the believer. You see, all truth in the Bible is germinated in Genesis. We find the seed plot of the Bible in the Book of Genesis, and we have the bud appearing there—much of the Bible is simply the unfolding. In Esau and Jacob we have a picture of the two natures in a believer today. If you are a child of God, you have a new nature—but you did not get rid of your old nature, and because of this there is conflict. The new nature and the old nature are opposed to each other. Paul said that the flesh wars against the Spirit, and the Spirit wars

4 *REAL CHARACTERS*

against the flesh. Esau pictures the flesh, Jacob pictures the spirit.

Esau, the man of the flesh, was outwardly far more attractive than Jacob. He was an outdoor man, the athletic type. He was the popular man, the extrovert, the *monsieur de monde*, the man of the world.

In contrast, Jacob was the man of the spirit—although that is not apparent at the beginning. When we first meet him he is actually much less attractive than Esau. He is clever, self-opinionated, crooked as can be, and above all he is mama's boy:

And Isaac loved Esau because he ate of his game, but Rebekah loved Jacob.
(Genesis 25:28)

In this family both parents had their favorites, which invariably creates friction. As we see these boys grow up we will notice that they were not identical twins—rather they were opposites. God said before they were born, so it would be of grace, "I have chosen the younger, and the older will serve him." Jacob, knowing God's promise, still connived for the right of the firstborn.

The birthright may not seem very important to you, but it actually meant that the boy possessing it would be the priest of the family, and it guaranteed that the promises made to the father would be confirmed to him. The ultimate promise was that the Messiah would come through the line of the one having the birthright. Esau, a man of the flesh, did not care about what might happen a thousand years from his day. He was not concerned about anything beyond his present life. His philosophy was eat, drink, and be merry, for tomorrow we die.

Esau came in from hunting, hungry—but not starving to death. Jacob did not take advantage of a starving man. Do you think anyone could have starved to death in the wealthy home of Abraham or Isaac? Of course not. But when he smelled the aroma of his brother's cooking, he wanted it. Now, you got nothing from Jacob unless you paid for it, and Jacob bargained, "I'll let you have it if you will let me have that birthright you don't care about." Esau so despised his birthright that he said, "You may have it, it means nothing to me." Thus Jacob buys that which God had already promised to give him—he wanted to get it on his own. God could not, nor did He, approve this transaction.

Jacob did not stop there. When old Isaac was about to do that which he should not have done—that is, bless Esau—the boy Jacob and his mother schemed. Actually they stole the blessing. Their father Isaac had said to Esau:

"And make me savory food, such as I love, and bring it to me that I may eat, that my soul may bless you before I die."
(Genesis 27:4)

Rebekah and Jacob collaborated in the deception:

Then Rebekah took the choice clothes of her elder son Esau, which were with her in the house, and put them on Jacob her younger son. And she put the skins of the kids of the goats on his hands and on the smooth part of his neck. Then she gave the

savory food and the bread, which she had
prepared, into the hand of her son Jacob.
So he went to his father and said, "My father." And he said, "Here I am. Who are you,
my son?" Jacob said to his father, "I am
Esau your firstborn; I have done just as you
told me; please arise, sit and eat of my game,
that your soul may bless me."
(Genesis 27:15–19)

Isaac, his senses dimmed by age, was taken in by this
clever ruse.

And he came near and kissed him; and he
smelled the smell of his clothing, and
blessed him and said:

"Surely, the smell of my son
Is like the smell of a field
Which the LORD has blessed.
Therefore may God give you
Of the dew of heaven,
Of the fatness of the earth,
And plenty of grain and wine.
Let peoples serve you,
And nations bow down to you.
Be master over your brethren,
And let your mother's sons bow down to
    you.
Cursed be everyone who curses you,
And blessed be those who bless you!"
(Genesis 27:27–29)

The theft of the blessing was the straw that broke the camel's back. It turned Jacob's brother against him:

**So Esau hated Jacob because of the bless-
ing with which his father blessed him, and
Esau said in his heart, "The days of mourn-
ing for my father are at hand; then I will kill
my brother Jacob."**
(Genesis 27:41)

My father is old, he thought, *and I don't want to do
anything that would put him in his grave; but the minute
he dies, I am going to kill my brother.*
Now when Rebekah heard about this threat to her
favorite son, she said to Jacob,

**"Now therefore, my son, obey my voice:
arise, flee to my brother Laban in Haran.
And stay with him a few days, until your
brother's fury turns away."**
(Genesis 27:43, 44)

She told him to go there for just a few days—but the
days lengthened into twenty years, and in the mean-
time Rebekah died. She never saw her boy again. Her
sin was judged.

THE ENCOUNTER

This boy leaves home and spends his first night out
at Bethel. That night he dreams of a ladder set up on
earth with angels on it. If I had written this account I
would have said that the angels came from heaven

descending, and then returned, ascending. But the record does not read that way. It states that the angels
were ascending and descending. What does that mean?
God is telling this boy that He will answer prayer. The
ascending angel, the prayer; the descending angel, the
answer—and the ladder is our Lord Jesus Christ.

In the New Testament, when Jesus called Nathanael,
He characterized him as "an Israelite indeed, in whom
is no deceit." He was no *Jacob*—none of his cleverness,
none of his crookedness, none of his self-opinionated-
ness. Nathanael was a sincere man who had questioned
the messiahship of Jesus. "Can anything good come out
of Nazareth?" he had wisecracked to Philip. But Jesus
said to him,

> **"Before Philip called you, when you were
> under the fig tree, I saw you." Nathanael
> answered and said to Him, "Rabbi, You are
> the Son of God! You are the King of Israel!"
> Jesus answered and said to him, "Because
> I said to you, 'I saw you under the fig tree,'
> do you believe? You will see greater things
> than these." And He [Jesus] said to him,
> "Most assuredly, I say to you, hereafter you
> shall see heaven open, and the angels of
> God ascending and descending upon the
> Son of Man."**
> (John 1:48–51)

Christ is the ladder, and when the boy Jacob
pillowed his head on the stones at Bethel with the
wild winds racing about him, he dreamed of that

ladder. He thought he had left God back home. Listen
to him:

> **Then Jacob awoke from his sleep and said,
> "Surely the LORD is in this place, and I did
> not know it."**
> (Genesis 28:16)

You see, though down deep Jacob has a spiritual nature,
he is a conniver and a schemer, depending on his own
wits and his own strength. He is far from God. This boy,
when he left home and escaped from Esau, probably
mopped his brow and said, "Goodbye, Esau. Goodbye,
God." He honestly thought he had left God back home.
But the first night out God has appeared to him. He is
telling this lonesome, homesick boy that there is grace
and mercy with God, that he still has access to God, his
prayers will be heard and his prayers will be answered.
God has not forsaken him.

In the section of Romans where Paul discusses the
nation of Israel, and especially this boy and his brother
Esau, he says something in chapter 10 that is quite
interesting:

> **But the righteousness of faith speaks in this
> way, "Do not say in your heart, 'Who will
> ascend into heaven?'" (that is, to bring
> Christ down from above).**
> (Romans 10:6)

You do not have to bring Christ down a ladder today.
He is available to you—right where you are sitting.

Or,

"'Who will descend into the abyss?'" (that is, to bring Christ up from the dead).
(Romans 10:7)

He is already back from the dead, my beloved.

But what does it say? "The word is near you, in your mouth and in your heart" (that is, the word of faith which we preach).
(Romans 10:8)

Such is the gospel which we preach today, the gospel of a ladder reaching to heaven. God is available. You do not have to go through a religious system, a church, or a preacher.

There is nothing between your soul and God. This is the frightening thing, and it is the thing that frightened Jacob. When you are running away from your brother because you have deceived him, when you are out of the will of God, such a discovery is frightening. God says to you and He says to me, "There is not even a tissue between your soul and Me. I am available." The Lord Jesus says, "I am the way, the ladder."

That if you confess with your mouth the Lord Jesus and believe in your heart that God has raised Him from the dead, you will be saved. For with the heart one believes unto righteousness, and with the mouth confession is made unto salvation.
(Romans 10:9, 10)

There is a ladder let down from heaven right where you

are at this moment. All you have to do is bring your mouth and your heart into harmony so that they say the same thing. Trust Christ as your personal Savior today. Believe that God gave Him for your sin and that God raised Him from the dead, and you will be saved. The way is wide open for you today. No man is able to open it, but Christ opened it for you about two thousand years ago. Christ is the ladder.

Jacob found that ladder when he ran away from home. And God promised to be with him. Imagine God promising to be with this clever, self-opinionated boy who thinks he knows everything!

"Behold, I am with you and will keep you wherever you go, and will bring you back to this land; for I will not leave you until I have done what I have spoken to you."
(Genesis 28:15)

God says, in essence, "I will not leave you, I will not forsake you. You did not run away from Me. I am going to continue to deal with you." Believe me, God dealt with this boy—which we shall see.

Notice the reaction of this runaway boy—I told you he was frightened. "And he was afraid and said, 'How awesome is this place!'" (v. 17).

You know, that is the reason some folk will not come to church or Bible study. They have a hundred excuses, but the real reason is they do not want to get that close to God. Actually the reason multitudes of folk want to go through a ceremony, a ritual, a church, or a man is so that they will not have to go firsthand to God. But by

Jesus' death and resurrection He cut out the middle-
man, and now you go to Him directly.

Listen to Jacob:

**"How awesome is this place! This is none
other than the house of God, and this is the
gate of heaven!"**
(Genesis 28:17)

This is Bethel, the house of God.

Such was his experience, and now he makes his vow.

**Then Jacob made a vow, saying, "If God will
be with me, and keep me in this way that I
am going, and give me bread to eat and
clothing to put on, so that I come back to my
father's house in peace, then the LORD shall
be my God."**
(Genesis 28:20, 21)

He can't help but trade! Even after God promises to do
it for him, he turns right around and says, *"If* God will
do this for me, then He will be my God"—always trad-
ing, always depending on himself to work something
out. However, this experience at Bethel is the high point
in his life. I believe it is his conversion.

ON TO HARAN

On to Haran now, on to the place where his mother,
Rebekah, had sent him—to her brother's home. Jacob
resumes his journey, cocksure, self-sufficient, conceited.
However, unbeknownst to him, he is moving toward

college—the college of hard knocks. His Uncle Laban is
dean and professor of all the courses, and, believe me,
he is a good teacher.

When Jacob arrives in Haran, he meets a girl. Rachel
comes to the well with her father's sheep. Jacob waters
the sheep, then (I have always been amused at this) he
kisses Rachel, and lifts his voice and weeps. It is love at
first sight. She is the only fine thing in this man's life. She
is at his side through all the hard years in Haran. After
many years they have a son, Joseph. Later Benjamin is
born at Bethlehem. His birth cost Rachel's life, and it is
at Bethlehem that Jacob buries his beautiful Rachel.

But, now, Jacob is a young fellow. He has just arrived
at Haran and has met Rachel. She leads him to her
home because she is the daughter of Uncle Laban. Jacob
doesn't know it, but he is in school now. Here he is, the
nephew who has come from a far country. But he is a
guest for only a few days. He had expected to be treated
in style. He had been able to outwit everybody, includ-
ing his father and his brother, but he encounters Uncle
Laban now, and Uncle Laban is smarter than he is.

One morning at breakfast Uncle Laban says,

**"Because you are my relative, should you
therefore serve me for nothing? Tell me,
what should your wages be?"**
(Genesis 29:15)

Laban sounds so magnanimous when he says, in effect,
"Although you are part of the family, I'm not going to
let you work here for nothing." Who said anything about
working? Jacob had not. He had not come to Haran to

work. That boy lived, not by the sweat of his brow and the rough hands of toil, but by his wits. Yet here somebody was getting in ahead of him. Uncle Laban says, "I'm not going to let you work for nothing, but tomorrow morning you're getting up with the other hired help and you are going to start working for me—and I'll pay you."

Now Laban had already seen Jacob eyeing Rachel. He knew what Jacob wanted, and he knew what he intended to give him. Jacob fell right into line, "I will serve you seven years for Rachel your younger daughter." The record gives us a brief glimpse into Jacob's heart during these years—"they seemed only a few days to him because of the love he had for her." Oh, how he loved her!

The seven years pass and Jacob comes to claim his beautiful bride, Rachel. An evening wedding is arranged, the bride comes out heavily veiled. The wedding night passes, and in the cruel light of day Jacob sees his bride—Leah!

But Laban is right there to explain everything. "I forgot to tell you, Jacob, that in our country it is the custom that the oldest daughter must be married first. I forgot to tell you that. You will have to take her first."

May I say to you, this boy is beginning to learn now. This is really his first big lesson. He refused submission to God at home, and he now must submit to his uncle in a far country. Jacob had deceived his father, he had stolen the blessing of the firstborn, now he has been deceived because of the right of the firstborn. He is learning the truth of the old saying, "Chickens come home to roost." They always do. And you will find that God puts it in different language later on:

Do not be deceived, God is not mocked; for whatever a man sows, that he will also reap. (Galatians 6:7)

Jacob deceived his old father about the favorite son. Many years later, when he himself was old, his own sons would bring to him the coat of Joseph—his favorite son—dipped in blood, the blood of goats, to deceive him into believing that his son had been slain. It is arresting to notice that every crooked thing this man did came back to him in the same coin. The Word of God promises that it will work that way.

After Jacob had been tricked into marrying Leah, he served seven more years to get Rachel. He served an additional six years to get his sheep. After dealing with Laban for twenty years, he took his leave—and Laban took out after him. Laban would have put him to death had not God intervened. When he caught up with Jacob he stormed, "What do you mean by taking my daughters and taking my grandchildren? You didn't even let me kiss them goodbye."

As Jacob defends his action, listen to his wail,

"Thus I have been in your house twenty years; I served you fourteen years for your two daughters, and six years for your flock, and you have changed my wages ten times." (Genesis 31:41)

Jacob is through at Haran now. He has had an excellent education and has finished all of Uncle Laban's courses.

HEADING HOME

Jacob resumes his journey, and one memorable night he is left alone to wrestle with God.

God is beginning to deal with Jacob directly in order to bring him into the place of fruit bearing and of real, vital service and witness for Him.

> **"Speak thus to my lord Esau, 'Thus your servant Jacob says: "I have dwelt with Laban and stayed there until now. . . . I have sent to tell my lord, that I may find favor in your sight."'"**
> (Genesis 32:4, 5)

He remembers the last time he saw Esau twenty years ago; Esau was breathing out threats against him. Notice that Jacob sends servants and instructs them, saying, "When you get to Esau my brother, say to him, 'My lord Esau.'" Of all things! And then he has them refer to himself as "your servant Jacob." That's not the way Jacob had spoken before. He had manipulated for the birthright and had stolen the blessing. He had been a rascal, but *now* his talk is different. I guess he had learned a few things from Uncle Laban. "My lord Esau . . . your servant Jacob."

> **Then the messengers returned to Jacob, saying, "We came to your brother Esau, and**

he also is coming to meet you, and four
hundred men are with him."
(Genesis 32:6)

This message absolutely frightened poor Jacob because he didn't know what all that meant. Esau did not
indicate his intentions to the servants at all. I suppose
that Jacob quizzed them rather thoroughly and said,
"Did you detect any note of animosity or bitterness or
hatred toward me?" And I suppose that one of the
servants said, "No, he seemed to be glad to get the
information that you were coming to meet him, and now
he's coming to meet you." But the fact that Esau appeared glad was no comfort to Jacob. It could mean that
Esau would be glad for the opportunity of getting re-
venge. Anyway, poor Jacob is upset.

**So Jacob was greatly afraid and distressed;
and he divided the people that were with
him, and the flocks and herds and camels,
into two companies.**
(Genesis 32:7)

He reasons that if his brother strikes one group, then
the other one can escape.

Notice what Jacob does now. He appeals to God in his
distress:

**Then Jacob said, "O God of my father Abra-
ham and God of my father Isaac, the LORD
who said to me, 'Return to your country and
to your family, and I will deal well with
you': I am not worthy of the least of all the**

mercies and of all the truth which You have shown Your servant; for I crossed over this Jordan with my staff, and now I have become two companies."
(Genesis 32:9, 10)

This man now appeals to God and cries out to Him on the basis that He is the God of his grandfather Abraham and the God of his father Isaac. I begin now to detect a little change in Jacob's life. This is the first time I have ever heard him say, "I am not worthy of the least of Your mercies." For the first time, he is acknowledging that he might be a sinner in God's sight. Do you know that there are a great many "Christians" who do not acknowledge that they are sinners? For years I knew a man who was incensed that I would indicate that he was a sinner. He told me all that he had done and that he had been saved and now was not a sinner. My friend, he is a sinner. We are all sinners, *saved by grace*. As long as we are in this life, we have that old nature that isn't even fit to go to heaven. When any man begins to move toward God on that basis, he will find that God will communicate with him.

That night Jacob sends all that he has across the Brook Jabbok, but he stays on the other side so that if his brother Esau comes he might kill Jacob but spare the family. And so Jacob is left alone.

Then Jacob was left alone; and a Man wrestled with him until the breaking of day.
(Genesis 32:24)

There are several things I would like to get straight as we come to this wrestling match. I have heard it said that Jacob did the wrestling. Actually, Jacob didn't want to wrestle anybody. He has Uncle Laban in back of him who doesn't mean good at all, and he has his brother Esau ahead of him. Jacob is no match for either one. He is caught now between a rock and a hard place, and he doesn't know which way to turn. Do you think he wanted to take on a third opponent that night? I don't think so.

This is the question: Who is this one who wrestled with Jacob that night? There has been a great deal of speculation about who it is, but I think He is none other than the preincarnate Christ.

Now when He saw that He did not prevail against him, He touched the socket of his hip; and the socket of Jacob's hip was out of joint as He wrestled with him.
(Genesis 32:25)

Jacob is not going to give up easily; he is not that kind of man—and he struggled against Him. Finally, this One who wrestled with him crippled him.

And He said, "Let Me go, for the day breaks." But he said, "I will not let You go unless You bless me!"
(Genesis 32:26)

What happens now? Jacob is just holding on; he's not wrestling. He is just holding on to this One. He found out that you do not get anywhere with God by struggling and resisting. The only way that you get anywhere with Him is by yielding and just holding on to Him. My friend, when you get in that condition, then you trust God. When you are willing to hold on, He is there ready to help you.

> **So He said to him, "What is your name?" He said, "Jacob." And He said, "Your name shall no longer be called Jacob, but Israel; for you have struggled with God and with men, and have prevailed."**
> (Genesis 32:27, 28)

He is not Jacob anymore—the one who is the usurper, the trickster—but Israel, "for you have struggled with God and with men, and have prevailed." Now the new nature of Israel will be manifested in the life of this man.

> **Then Jacob asked, saying, "Tell me Your name, I pray." And He said, "Why is it that you ask about My name?" And He blessed him there. So Jacob called the name of the place Peniel: "For I have seen God face to face, and my life is preserved."**
> (Genesis 32:29, 30)

Jacob had seen the Angel of the Lord, the pre-incarnate Christ.

> **Just as he crossed over Penuel the sun rose on him, and he limped on his hip.**
> (Genesis 32:31)

God had to cripple Jacob in order to get him, but He got him. This man Jacob refused to give in at first—that was typical of him. He knew a few holds, and he thought that after a while he would be able to overcome. Finally, he found out he couldn't overcome, but he would not surrender. And so what did God do? Certainly, with His superior strength, in a moment God could have pinned down Jacob's shoulders—but He wouldn't have pinned down his *will*. Jacob was like the little boy whose mama made him sit in a corner in his room. After a while she heard a noise in there and she called to him, "Willie, are you sitting down?" He said, "Yes, I'm sitting down, but I'm standing up on the inside of me!" That is precisely what would have happened to Jacob. He would have been standing up on the inside of himself—he wasn't ready to yield.

Notice how God deals with him. He touches the hollow of Jacob's thigh. Just a touch of the finger of God, and this man becomes helpless. But you see, God is not pinning down his shoulders. Now Jacob holds on to Him. The Man says, "Let Me go," and Jacob says, "No, I want Your blessing." He is clinging to God now. The struggling and striving are over, and from here on Jacob is going to manifest a spiritual nature, dependence upon God. You will not find the change happening in a moment's notice. Before we are through with him, we will find that he is a real man of God.

The next day Jacob meets Esau and discovers that his brother is not angry at all. Thus Esau reveals himself to be a bigger man than Jacob. Esau invites him to make his home with him, but Jacob does not want to live near his brother. He has something else in mind.

As soon as Esau has turned his back and started home, Jacob takes his family down to Shechem. It is a tragic move—Jacob is still depending on his own cleverness. There Dinah, his daughter by Leah, is raped. Then Simeon and Levi, her full brothers, go into the city of Shechem and to the prince who is responsible. Though the prince wants to marry Dinah, they murder him, and the sons of Jacob conduct a slaughter that would make a Mafia shooting in Chicago look pretty tame! When they come home, Jacob says, "You've made my name to stink among the people of this land." He should not have gone to Shechem. But he learned his lesson.

Some believers have yet to learn that sin will catch up with them. It always does. God said this in Galatians 6:7, 8:

For whatever a man sows, that he will also reap. For he who sows to his flesh will of the flesh reap corruption, but he who sows to the Spirit will of the Spirit reap everlasting life.

You sow corn, you reap corn; you sow wheat, you reap wheat; you sow cotton, you reap cotton; you sow sin, you reap sin. You reap exactly what you sow. Old Jacob, when he left Shechem a brokenhearted man, knew then that whatever a man sows he will reap.

BACK TO BETHEL

God called Jacob back to Bethel, back to a fresh start, a new era:

Then God said to Jacob, "Arise, go up to Bethel and dwell there; and make an altar there to God, who appeared to you when you fled from the face of Esau your brother." And Jacob said to his household and to all who were with him, "Put away the foreign gods that are among you, purify yourselves, and change your garments."
(Genesis 35:1, 2)

Rachel, you may recall, had taken the idols from her parental home and had concealed them while Laban searched the entire camp. I suppose she continued to worship those idols, for she had come from a home of idolatry. Jacob loved her and was too indulgent with her. It seems that idolatry was an accepted part of family life. Now God says, "Go back to Bethel. That's where I started with you, Jacob. You have to go back."

You have to be clean. That means confession of sins. My friend, you have to deal with sin in your life. Don't think that you can just rub out the sins of the past. You are dealing with God. You've got to confess your sin. God has said, "If we confess our sins, He is faithful and just to forgive us our sins and to cleanse us from all unrighteousness" (1 John 1:9). He can cleanse you today. You cannot go back to Bethel unless you clean up. That is what it means.

Then, "change your garments." *Garments* in Scripture are habits. We use the same expression today when we speak of riding habits or golfing habits. Jacob is God's man, he is going to change his garments, his habits, and start living differently. And as far as I can tell, from the day he went back to Bethel he started living for God.

Jacob said to his family,

"Then let us arise and go up to Bethel; and I will make an altar there to God, who answered me in the day of my distress and has been with me in the way which I have gone."
(Genesis 35:3)

He remembered that as a boy running away from home, homesick and lonesome, he had come to Bethel and God had appeared to him. God had said, "I'll be faithful to you." But Jacob had gone on his way, not depending on God's faithfulness but on his own ability. He fell on his face; disappointment and tragedy came to him. Yet through it all God was with him, and God blessed him. Now He says, "Go back to Bethel. You have to go back to where you started, Jacob. You have to go back."

YOUR BETHEL

How about you, my friend? Do you have a Bethel in your past? Do you remember the day you came to Christ? It was exciting, wasn't it! You were filled with wonder. Thrilling times those were! You may have wandered far since then. You may be at this moment actually away from God, living by your own wits, trusting in your own ability. Perhaps your life even blends in with the lives of those in the world.

Yet in spite of it all, God has blessed. Remember how it was with you at the beginning? You may not have had much then, materially speaking, but you had fellowship with your God. I call you back to Bethel today, back to the House of God.

Put away your idols.

You may protest, "You're wrong, preacher, we don't have any idols." Are you sure you don't? Materialism and secularism are our idols today. To some of you, your home is your idol—you have spent more in redecorating your home this past year than you have spent for God's work. And at the same time, you speak of looking for the Lord to come. Your neighbors know you don't mean it.

Some have made pleasure an idol. Actually, your interest in the church is in the entertainment it offers. You do not go to pray, you do not go to study the Word of God—you go to be entertained. Some of you have made television your god. You spend more time there on Sunday nights than you spend in the House of God. To some of you, business has become your idol and you have no time for your God. Some of you have made a child or your family or even church activity your idol. Good things, you know, can keep you from the best things.

Put away your strange gods if you are going back to Bethel. Be clean. There will have to be confession of sin. Change your garments—change your habits. Come back to Bethel, the House of God, back to the ladder which is Christ, through whom we have access to God, fellowship with Him.

So Jacob came to Luz (that is, Bethel), which is in the land of Canaan, he and all the people who were with him. And he built

an altar there and called the place El Bethel, because there God appeared to him when he fled from the face of his brother.

Then God appeared to Jacob again, when he came from Padan Aram, and blessed him. And God said to him, "Your name is Jacob; your name shall not be called Jacob anymore, but Israel shall be your name." So He called his name Israel.

Then God went up from him in the place where He talked with him. So Jacob set up a pillar in the place where He talked with him, a pillar of stone; and he poured a drink offering on it, and he poured oil on it. And Jacob called the name of the place where God spoke with him, Bethel.
(Genesis 35:6, 7, 9, 10, 13–15)

— 2 —
JOSHUA
The Man God Can Use

Moses had gone to the top of Mount Nebo and he had not returned.

The Book of Deuteronomy closes by saying, as one translation has it, "He died by the kiss of God." It was not the kiss of death. Rather, God kissed this tired, weary servant of His and put him to bed, for Moses had for forty years led and borne with the children of Israel. I do not believe that any man has ever been called upon to undergo any more hardship than this man Moses had. He is one of the great men of this earth.

Moses was a man of remarkable ability, and he also was what Napoleon called "a man of destiny." That is, certain men appear at certain strategic moments in the history of this world, and certainly Moses was that kind of man. But now he'd gone to the top of the mountain, and he had not come down. As the poet has put it:

By Nebo's lonely mountain
   On this side Jordan's wave
In a vale in the land of Moab,
   There lies a lonely grave.

And no man knows that sepulchre,
   And no man saw it e'er
For the angels of God upturned the sod,
   And laid the dead man there.

> —Cecil Frances Alexander
> "The Burial of Moses"

Now who would be the successor to Moses? As we look over the field, who could qualify for his position?

WHO CAN GOD USE?

Actually, there was no man of the caliber of Moses upon the horizon. The most likely candidate for the office was, first of all, Caleb. Caleb was an older man than Joshua. He was a man of riper experience, and that which we do know about him reveals that he was a greater leader than Joshua. And then there was a second man, Phinehas, the son of Moses. He would have been the natural successor to Moses.

But the very interesting thing is that God bypassed both of these men, and He chose Joshua, an ordinary man. And I suspect that Joshua, least of all, thought that he would be called. I do not believe that he felt he was to follow in Moses' line. He was what Dr. Blackwood said years ago: "Joshua is a demonstration of what God can do with an average man when he is completely yielded to Him."

Now this man Joshua was definitely an average man. Why did God overlook better-qualified applicants? Why did He settle for Joshua, the common vegetable variety of a man, in any sense a very colorless individual? Did you know, friend, that it has always been the policy of God to choose men of this type? God never chooses the strongest. Note His rule, as Paul stated it, that we don't find written down until we come to the New Testament:

For you see your calling, brethren, that not many wise according to the flesh, not many mighty, not many noble, are called. But God has chosen the foolish things of the world to put to shame the wise, and God has chosen the weak things of the world to put to shame the things which are mighty; and the base things of the world and the things which are despised God has chosen, and the things which are not, to bring to nothing things that are, that no flesh should glory in His presence.
(1 Corinthians 1:26–29)

Even in the case of Moses you will find that he was too strong for God to use. After forty years of training in the palace in Egypt in preparation for becoming the next Pharaoh, evidently educated in the Temple of the Sun, a man who had an education that would compare favorably to any university graduate today, this man Moses was too strong for God to use. So God put him out on the backside of the desert in Midian! For another forty years God let this man herd sheep, until he came to the place where he would say, "Who am I that I should go to Pharaoh, and that I should bring the children of Israel out of Egypt?" (Exodus 3:11). In other words, he said, "I'm not able to do the job." And when he said that, God said, "You are now able to do the job."

You see, that is the problem that God has with most of us. We are too strong for God to use us. God usually chooses for a particular task a man who has some weakness. Have you ever noticed it in Scripture? Gideon was the least in his father's house, but God used him. David was just a little shepherd boy whom his own father overlooked, never dreaming that God could use him. But David is the one God chose. Elijah and Jeremiah were strong prophets, yet these were very weak men underneath. One of them wanted to commit suicide and the other man wanted to resign. They both begged off and said in essence, "We don't want the job you have given us." But those were the men God used.

Paul himself made the statement that he was not eloquent enough for a personal appearance, and yet God said, "You are to appear before kings for Me," and God used him in that way (see Mark 13:9). May I say that these are the types of men God has always used. Simon Peter was a man like that. He said to our Lord, "Depart from me, for I am a sinful man," which conveys the thought, "Why don't You go on and get somebody else? I've failed You so many times!" But the Lord Jesus said, "Do not be afraid. From now on you will catch men" (Luke 5:8, 10). He was saying, "It's because you don't think you can do it that I can use you."

The great problem in the church in our day is we have too many people who have talent and ability. They feel that God can and will use that. But He doesn't use that primarily. Instead He chooses a person who is mediocre, a weak person.

Let me ask you a very personal question. Have you ever wondered why God has not used you in a wider way? I say it cordially, but I say it candidly, we are too strong for God to use us. We are just too strong. We have too much ability and we have too much talent for God to use us. We have our own plans and our own programs. Many of these young people who have graduated from high school and college already have their life plans made, and they are asking God to rubber stamp them. Do you have your heart set for the future? Are you self-sufficient but hoping that God will come in and bless periodically—especially if you get in a tight place—but you don't want Him running the affair? You don't want Him really to take charge. And there is one thing for sure—you do not want Him to alter or change your plans. You just want Him to bless them, that is all.

May I say to you that Joshua was the man that God could use, and he was only an average man. But Joshua was better equipped than he thought he was. God had been preparing him to succeed Moses. There is, I believe, a law of life with God—that you and I learn obedience through the things that we suffer—and many of us haven't suffered in the past few years. Therefore we have not brought our wills nor even our thoughts into captivity to Jesus Christ.

Now let's look at Joshua. This man had shared for forty years the heartbreak of the wilderness. He had *wandered* forty years when he wanted to *march*! And Joshua was ready to march. He was one of the twelve spies who was sent into the Promised Land to see what it was like and what kind of people lived there, then to bring back a report. He brought back an enthusiastic report and said, "Let's go in and possess the land." But the people of Israel said no, and this man had to turn his back on the Promised Land and stay out in that terrible wilderness. And for forty years it was heartbreak for him, but he learned obedience by the things that he suffered. He had to wait forty years for patience, long years of training and preparation. And Moses, if you'll notice toward the end of his life, began to realize that God was training this man Joshua. He saw that this ordinary man—the man who was only a face in the great sea of faces of those who had come out of Egypt— this man was being trained by God for this particular office of leadership.

What is God educating you for today? Do you fret at your lot in life? Do you chafe under the circumstances in which you find yourself? Did you know that our bitter experiences become our sweetest experiences? There is a truth our Lord gave which He will follow right to the letter, even in a space age: we must suffer if we are to reign with Him. He will not depart from that even today. What is God educating you for and training you for?

Now think of this man Joshua whom God had trained. He had been born in the land of Egypt, born a slave. He was around forty years old at the time of the Exodus, a young man, and for forty years he went through that wilderness march. At the end of that second forty years, God put the mantle of Moses upon him. He was the man God chose to follow Moses.

Joshua knew his own weakness. Joshua knew the limit of his ability, and you will find that in the first chapter of the Book of Joshua God moves in on this man. Three times He said to him, "Be strong and of good courage." Why did He say that? Because Joshua was not strong, because he was absolutely cowardly. When he looked across that Jordan River, he could see the well-fortified city of Jericho and the enemies throughout the land, and *he* had been chosen to lead over there this great company of God's people! May I say to you, he needed the encouragement that only God could give him.

Now the time had come to cross over into the land which God had promised. It was April, about 1400 B.C., the Jordan River was at flood stage, and God brought the people of Israel over the river by a miracle.

So it was, when the people set out from their camp to cross over the Jordan, with the priests bearing the ark of the covenant before the people, and as those who bore the ark came to the Jordan, and the feet of the priests who bore the ark dipped in the edge of the water (for the Jordan overflows all its banks during the whole time of harvest), that the waters which came down from upstream stood still, and rose in a heap very far away at Adam, the city that is beside Zaretan. So the waters that went down into the Sea of the Arabah, the Salt Sea, failed, and were cut off; and the people crossed over opposite Jericho. Then the priests who bore the ark of the covenant of the LORD stood firm on dry ground in the midst of the Jordan; and all Israel crossed

over on dry ground, until all the people had crossed completely over the Jordan.
(Joshua 3:14–17)

It was just as great a miracle as there had been at the Red Sea.

Certainly after this experience Joshua was encouraged. They came to Gilgal and camped there while circumcision was performed. This rolled away the reproach of Egypt so that the people of Israel could enter as God's chosen people into the land He had given them. The manna which had fed them in the wilderness had now ceased. The wilderness march is over, the years of wandering have come to an end. There is a new regime, and there is a new generation. They are ready to march in, and the city of Jericho is shut up tight. There is a great feeling of anticipation in the air, and this man— this average man—is under severe strain and tension at this time. Therefore he has another lesson to learn, and God is going to teach him this tremendous lesson before he enters into his work of conquering that land for God.

There is always a danger for an average man—when promoted to a high position—of being filled with pride, especially if he has been successful to a certain degree. And certainly Joshua had been successful in the sense that the children of Israel had triumphantly crossed over the Jordan River. Though it had not been accomplished through his ability or his strength, he was the leader.

Now what is the secret of Joshua's success? The answer to that question is the subject of this message and is an important one, as we shall see.

Joshua came out of his tent one morning after they had crossed over the Jordan River. And when he came out, I think he was walking with the pride of a second lieutenant. Did you ever meet any of those fellows? May I say that no Caesar ever walked with the pride of a second lieutenant, and I do not believe that anyone ever walked with more pride than Joshua felt that morning when he came out of his tent. He stopped to survey the encampment of Israel—a sight to behold! There was the tabernacle in the center, with the pillar of cloud above, and the children of Israel encamped in an orderly fashion around it, as they had been encamping for forty years in the wilderness. It was a sight that caused Balaam, yonder on top of a mountain, to say, "How goodly are thy tents, oh Israel." It certainly caused Joshua to burst open a few buttons on his uniform. *To think, I am now in charge here! Moses is buried on the other side of the Jordan River, and now I'm in charge.*

But Joshua saw something out there that disturbed him. Will you notice what he saw:

And it came to pass, when Joshua was by Jericho, that he lifted his eyes and looked, and behold, a Man stood opposite him with His sword drawn in His hand. And Joshua went to Him and said to Him, "Are You for us or for our adversaries?"
(Joshua 5:13)

He saw a man down yonder at the edge of the camp with a sword drawn! Apparently there was somebody there who didn't know that he was General Joshua and that he had not given an order for anybody to draw a sword. So he strides down to where this one is standing with a drawn sword, and he says to him, "Are you for us or for our enemies?" Or, if you want it in the common colloquialism of the street, "What's the big idea of drawing a sword? Don't you know who is in command here?"

Then that One turned. Notice this in verse 14: "So He said, 'No, but as Commander of the army of the LORD I have now come.'" And Joshua saw who it was. It was the Angel of the Lord! And I want you to look at Joshua's instant reaction: "And Joshua fell on his face to the earth and worshiped, and said unto Him, 'What does my Lord say to His servant?'" May I say to you that this One, who is called the Angel of the Lord, I believe to be none other than the preincarnate Christ! When He turned and faced Joshua, the lesson he learned in that instant was this: General Joshua was not the one in command, and General Headquarters was not in his tent. General Headquarters was in heaven. Somebody else was in charge, and Joshua was not the one giving orders. Instead he was to follow orders. What a lesson!

> **Then the Commander of the LORD's army said to Joshua, "Take your sandal off your foot, for the place where you stand is holy." And Joshua did so.**
> (Joshua 5:15)

General Joshua obeyed because he has now learned that there is Someone else giving orders, and he is merely following orders.

The Captain of the host of the Lord is the One who was there. I said I believe He was the preincarnate Christ. I do not intend to belabor that point, but may I say that when you come to the New Testament, there is no question who the Captain of our salvation is. In the Epistle to the Hebrews, speaking of the Lord Jesus Christ and of His humanity, the record reads:

For it was fitting for Him, for whom are all things and by whom are all things, in bringing many sons to glory, to make the captain of their salvation perfect through sufferings.
(Hebrews 2:10)

The Captain of our salvation has come down and taken upon Himself our human flesh. He knew what it was to be a soldier of God down here on earth. He went through basic training here. He knew what it was to take orders when He was here in His humanity. He said, "I have come to do what the Father tells Me to do. I do not do My own will, but the will of the Father who sent Me." Now He has gone back to His rightful place. The writer to the Hebrews says, "He is the Captain of our salvation." This does not mean that He only saved us—it means today that He is the One who is giving the orders!

Will you notice again in the Epistle to the Hebrews:

Therefore we also, since we are surrounded by so great a cloud of witnesses, let us lay aside every weight, and the sin which so easily ensnares us, and let us run with endurance the race that is set before us, look-

ing unto Jesus, the author [Captain] **and finisher of our faith.**
(Hebrews 12:1, 2a)

It says the *author*, but it is the same word that's translated "captain" in chapter 2, and I think it should be Captain here—"Looking unto Jesus, the Captain of our salvation."

This moment, right now, our Lord is in heaven at God's right hand, and He is still the Captain. Headquarters for the church is still up there, not down here. No one down here gives orders; He still gives the orders. That is something we seem to have forgotten. We are privates, buck privates in the rear rank. He gives the orders. We are to obey. And may I again say this, here is where most of us fail in finding the will of God for our lives. We forget that He gives the orders.

HOW TO KNOW THE WILL OF GOD

The will of God for our lives, for your life and for my life, is to obey Christ. I had the privilege one night of speaking to the graduating class at Culter Academy. That meant more to me than anything else I had done in years, and I spoke along this line, how you can know the will of God for your life. And I do not care where you read in the Word of God, you will find that those who did the will of God followed these simple suggestions. They are really simple, and I'd like to make them very brief.

There must first of all be on our part a recognition that Jesus Christ has a right to our lives. May I say that Joshua didn't even raise that question. When he went to find out who this was who was not obeying him and

discovered that it was the Captain of the host of the
Lord, Joshua immediately changed and became a buck
private, and you'll find him being obedient. He fell at
the feet of this One and said to Him, "What do You want
me to do? I'm Your servant, I'm the buck private—You
tell me what to do." And, my friend, may I say to you
that I don't think the Lord had a bit of trouble causing
the walls of Jericho to fall down. But there is something
that always did bother me. How could He get that crowd
of fighting men to march around the walls for seven
consecutive days and do nothing else? And if you had
met General Joshua on the first day after they had
marched around once and returned to the camp and
said, "General Joshua, you didn't make an attack today!" He would have answered, "No, we didn't."

"When are you going to attack?"

"I don't know."

"You mean to tell me you are general here and you
don't know—you don't have your strategy?"

"Strategies come from up yonder."

"General Joshua, don't you know it's foolish for an
army not to attack?"

"Sure, I know it's foolish."

"Well, General Joshua, don't you feel pretty silly?"

"I feel ridiculous!"

"Then why in the world are you doing it?"

"I'm following orders, and don't you know that a
soldier follows orders?"

My friend, there must be on our part an honest
recognition that Jesus Christ is in charge of our lives.
This is not something theoretical that I'm talking to
you about today. This is practical, and I do not mean

only on Sundays. There are a great many folks who say, "Yes, He has a right to my life, and you know, every Sunday I go down to that church and I really work." Somebody else says, "Yes, I believe He has a right to my life, and when I was elected to an office, I prayed about it and I want you to know that I recognize He has a right to my life." You do? Do you believe today that He has a right to every moment of your life, that when you go to work tomorrow morning He is still the General, He is still the Commander-in-Chief, He is still the One to give you orders—not only for some particular service that you're going to do sometime, but all the time, every moment?

Often I think of the story told about Count Zinzendorff when he went to one of his Moravian brethren one day. They were very much mission-minded, as you may know, and he said to this brother, "Can you go to the mission field?" The fellow said, "Yes."

"Can you go today?"

"Well, yes, just as soon as I get my shoes down at the shoe shop."

If Jesus Christ gave you orders like that today, would you follow them? Would you? Then don't talk about His will for your life. If you think He's going to rubber stamp your well-planned life, you are wrong. He's not in that business.

Now we recognize that others have a right to our lives. We recognize that our family makes demands on us. And you'll probably be at your place of business right on the dot in the morning. Why? Because that business makes a demand on you. Most of us recognize that our friends have a right to some of our time, and even our churches have certain rights. What about Jesus Christ? I'm not talking about rights in a general sort of way, but I'm talking about a total commitment to Him, so that when He tells you to do anything, you will do it.

When I was pastor in Nashville, Tennessee, I was single, and the fellow I had worked with when I was in the bank got into a lot of trouble. In fact, he called me one night and said he was contemplating suicide, and would I come over and talk to him. I went over and I talked with him for a couple of hours and got him to promise that he would not commit suicide. I said to him when I left, "Look, now you call me anytime you want to—at twelve o'clock at night or two or five o'clock in the morning—or anytime of the day. Regardless of what I'm doing, I'll talk to you. If I'm preaching in the pulpit and you send me word, I'll cut the sermon short and I'll come to you." And I meant it, and I did it. But I ask myself now, can Jesus Christ make that kind of demand of me today? Can He make that kind of demand of you today? There must be a recognition that Jesus Christ has a right to our lives.

Second, *there must be a realization that He wants something of us.* To me, the most amazing thing—and this has always thrilled me from the very beginning—is that He can take our feeble, spoiled, helpless, mixed-up lives and He can use us, and He actually *wants* to do that.

Now somebody says, "Yes, God wanted Abraham, I read that account and know He wanted Abraham. I read the story of Moses, and I'm sure He wanted Moses. And Joshua—even though he was an ordinary man, I can see that He wanted Joshua. And I can see He wanted David. He wanted Saul of Tarsus, waylaid him on the Damascus Road, and got him. But I don't know, does He want me?" May I say to you, He wants you just the same way, just the same way.

During World War II in the post offices and in certain other public places there was that picture of Uncle Sam, very stern, pointing his finger, and the caption was, "Uncle Sam wants *you!*" Did you ever see that one? That's the way Jesus Christ is pointing at you today. He wants you!

Joshua knew he was ordinary, he knew he was average, but he also recognized that God wanted something of him. And Jesus Christ wants something of you today.

Now I come to the third condition: *There must be a determination on our part to know the will of God.* Make a definite effort to find out what it is. I've always wanted to ask Joshua about that trip he made around Jericho seven straight days, and I intend to talk to him about it someday. I do not know what he's going to say, but I think one of the things he's going to say is this, "When God put His hand on me, and I knew that I had taken Moses' place, I was determined to know what God's will was for me, and I was determined to do it. I'm not sure, but maybe the reason He made me march around Jericho as a general for seven days was to make me know that I was seeking the will of God."

I had a preacher friend in Texas years ago who told me about a woman who came to him, and she said, "Do you believe that God tells you every thirty minutes what He wants you to do in that half hour?" And he said to her, "No, I don't believe it the way you want it to sound. I don't believe it that way at all."

"Well," she said, "I want you to know this, that every thirty minutes God tells me what to do. Do you believe it?"

He said, "Yes, I believe it, but it's not God that tells you, it's the demons of Satan who are telling you. God doesn't reveal His will that way."

God's orders are here in the Bible. One of the reasons today that many of us are having problems and difficulties is we just haven't read the orders yet. He is not speaking anywhere else. It is a lot more difficult to read and study this Book than it is to go around and say that you are having a vision or that you dreamed something or you had a little brief prayer meeting. But I do believe that through His Word and through prayer God reveals His will to us.

I come now to the final and the last condition for knowing God's will, and this is really the hard one: *There must be a day-by-day yielding to do what He lays on our hearts.* And I believe God desires to make it very clear what He wants us to do. Our problem is that we wait until we get to a crisis in our lives, and then we go to Him and call upon Him. It's like when you put a spare tire in your car—you hope you never have to use it but, boy, you are glad you've got it when you have a flat out on the freeway! And many of us, when crisis comes in our lives, go to God and say, "O Lord, I've graduated from school now. Tell me what to do, because I am in a crisis!" "I've lost my job." Or "the market went down, I'm having problems, Lord, help me out now." And then we wonder why He doesn't flash it on the screen.

May I say to you that Joshua was born a slave in Egypt. Then for forty years he had walked in obedience to God in that wilderness. Every day he looked longingly over into the Promised Land and he said, "Lord, I'd like to go over today," and God said, "Not today." He said, "Yes, Sir," and he marched on. It wasn't any new departure for Joshua to yield to this Captain of the host of the Lord. He had been doing it all his life.

GETTING DOWN TO BUSINESS

You can settle in the next ten seconds your status as a Christian and how to know the will of God for your life. Do you believe it? Let me ask just this one question now: Is the Lord Jesus Christ the Captain of *your* salvation? "Oh," you say, "He saved me. I came to Him and trusted Him as my Savior." But, my friend, He died nearly 2,000 years ago, and today He is at God's right hand and He is still giving orders. Is He your *Captain* now?

A young man sat in a congregation listening to a little-known preacher by the name of Henry Varley. He wasn't even a good preacher. But Henry Varley said, "The world has yet to see what God can do with a man who is fully yielded to Him." Dwight L. Moody, that young man sitting out there, said, "By the grace of God I'm going to be that man." In my book he was that man. But when Dwight L. Moody was dying, he said, "I heard Henry Varley when I was a young man say, 'The world has yet to see what God can do with a man who is fully yielded to Him.' And I said I'd be that man, but the world has *yet* to see what God can do with a man who is fully yielded to Him."

We are playing at church, aren't we? Honestly now, are you shortchanging Jesus Christ? When I go upstairs to my room after delivering this message today and look in the mirror, I'll say, "What you said just now goes double for you." Let's not play around, let's mean business with Him. Is Jesus Christ the Commander-in-Chief of your life today? Are you in the will of God this day? Are you obeying Him? Let's pray.

Our gracious loving Father God, we bow before Thee as we search our own hearts and look back on our lives. We know today that we've been out of step. We know that we have not been marching according to orders, that we are living our own selfish lives, insisting on our own way, taking the easy course. We're attempting to salve it over and call it the will of God. Lord, help us to come out from behind our false front, our facade of piosity. O help us, as Joshua, to bow to You and say to the Captain of our salvation, "You give the orders and I'll follow; I'll obey." Speak to my heart. I pray in Jesus' name, Amen.

— 3 —
CALEB

The Man Who Found the Fountain of Youth

The Word of God contains a great many little-known big men. They are unknown and unsung, and some of God's choicest saints have received scant attention on the pages of Scripture. Caleb is one of these great men of the Word of God. Caleb is on a par with Joshua—he was equally as great a man. Candidly, I do not understand why God chose Joshua and did not choose Caleb to follow Moses, because Caleb seems to have had just as many qualifications and was just as much committed to God as Joshua was.

Caleb was a great man of faith. Now I know that someone will say, "Well, when you go to the eleventh chapter of Hebrews and read the list of the heroes of faith, Caleb is not mentioned." Actually, Caleb is not mentioned at all in the New Testament. But I believe there's a reason that his name is omitted in the eleventh chapter of Hebrews. The writer tells us very cogently why he left out certain ones: "for the time would fail me." He said in effect, "I can't go back into the Old Testament and give you the entire catalog of the heroes of faith. God keeps that record up yonder." And I know one thing, Caleb's name is on God's list of heroes of faith. He was a man of faith. And we find here, in Joshua 14:11, his statement:

"As yet I am as strong this day as on the day that Moses sent me; just as my strength was then, so now is my strength for war, both for going out and for coming in."

Now this man somehow or another found the fountain of youth! Forty years in the wilderness was quite an experience, by the way. He and Joshua are the only ones of their generation who made it through the wilderness, yet he could say, "I'm as strong this day as I was forty years ago when I came into this land to spy it out." Not many men can say that, but this man could. He was a man of faith.

Ponce de Leon came with Columbus on his second trip to the Western Hemisphere, and Ponce de Leon was looking for the fountain of youth. He looked all over Florida and didn't find it, and of course we understand why. He was looking in the wrong place! But nevertheless, this man had to confess he had not found it.

LaSalle went across the country looking for the same thing. And he found the upper Mississippi. Instead of finding the fountain of youth he found Old Man River.

Certainly these men did not find the fountain of youth, but here is a man who did. Caleb was forty years old when he left the land of Egypt where he had been a slave—that was rigorous. Then he had spent forty years in the wilderness, which was even more so, and now the man says, "I'm as strong as I was when I was a young man forty years of age." What had happened? Well, he found the fountain of youth.

I'd like for us to search out Caleb's secret as he searched out the land forty years before. I want you to look at three things concerning this man. First, he had faith to forget the past. Second, he had faith to face the facts of the present. And third, there was faith to face the future. These are three wonderful qualities for any person to have. I do not guarantee they will keep you young, but I do say this: whether you are young or old, or whether you live to a ripe old age or die in youth, they will contribute to a joyful and fruitful Christian life.

FAITH TO FORGET THE PAST

Now first of all, let's note faith to forget the past. And I want to turn back to the Book of Numbers where we were first introduced to this man. In Numbers we were told that Caleb was one of the twelve spies who was chosen to go into the land, look it over, and bring back a report. So they secretly spied out the land, came back, and all of the spies reported their findings. When they were dealing with the facts, all gave the same report. They said that it was a land that was flowing with milk and honey, that it was a land that was a delightful place, that it was a land of fruit and grain, and it was every-thing God had said it was. You see, they didn't need to spy it out. They could have taken God's word for it because when they got back they had no new information. They were even told by the Lord about the giants! But when these spies saw the giants they were frightened. And when they got to the interpretation of the facts, that's when the reports differed, and we find a majority report and a minority report. The majority report said let's not go in; we can't take the land. And humanly speaking, they could not take the land.

But I want you to listen to this man Caleb, for up to this point there has been no leader except Moses. And my reason for believing Caleb was an outstanding man is that he was the one, not Joshua, who stepped forward here at the beginning.

> **Then Caleb quieted the people before Moses, and said, "Let us go up at once and take possession, for we are well able to overcome it." But the men who had gone up with him said, "We are not able to go up against the people, for they are stronger than we."**
> (Numbers 13:30, 31)

Of course, that was true, but Caleb was a man of faith, if you please, and he knew God had promised to give them the land. This man Caleb was ready to go in. He had faith to go in and take the land.

But the people of Israel at this time forgot all about the Promised Land and turned their thoughts back to Egypt. And we read,

**So they said to one another, "Let us select
a leader and return to Egypt."**
(Numbers 14:4)

The children of Israel wanted to go back to Egypt.
They said, "Those brickyards weren't near as bad as
we thought they were. The taskmaster's lash on our
back—we've forgotten about it—it wasn't as bad as we
thought it was. We want to go back." But Caleb, he
had faith to forget the past. He had faith to forget
Egypt. He had faith to turn his back upon that which
was in the past.

Now will you notice, that is what the Bible says,

**But Joshua the son of Nun and Caleb the
son of Jephunneh, who were among those
who had spied out the land, tore their
clothes; and they spoke to all the congregation of the children of Israel, saying: "The
land we passed through to spy out is an
exceedingly good land. If the LORD delights
in us, then He will bring us into this land
and give it to us, 'a land which flows with
milk and honey.' Only do not rebel against
the LORD, nor fear the people of the land,
for they are our bread; their protection has
departed from them, and the LORD is with
us. Do not fear them."**
(Numbers 14:6–9)

If you want that in good old American, he said, "They're
duck soup for us. We won't have any difficulty taking

this land for the very simple reason that God has promised it to us, and we can lay hold of it."

Now Caleb has broken all ties with Egypt. He has now turned his back on the past. Our Lord made the statement that it is a dangerous thing to put your hand to the plow and look back—we are to keep on going. I say to you today, if God has led you to make a certain decision and you have started following along—especially if you are a young person—and you come to a place where you're seeing giants now and feel timid about going ahead, oh, have faith to forget the past. Break with that. Don't go back to where you were. Keep pressing on!

May I say that this injunction is for all of us. When we put our hand to the plow, we need to keep going and not look back. The Lord Jesus said to the man who had been physically helpless for thirty-eight years yonder at the pool of Bethesda, "Rise, take up your bed and walk" (John 5:8). Why take up his bed? He won't be coming back here. As the Puritan commentator said, "The Lord told him to take up his bed because he was to make no arrangement for a relapse." Let somebody else have his place.

There are a great many Christians today who, when they start out, have made all their plans for a return trip. The fact of the matter is, they did not buy a one-way ticket in the will of God. You and I need to forget the past, put it behind us. Paul could say, "One thing I do." The reason so many of us are frustrated is because we haven't sharpened our lives down to that one thing: "[This] one thing I do, forgetting those things which are behind . . . " (Philippians 3:13*a*).

Memory is a wonderful thing. It gives you roses in December. But do you know that forgetting is equally as wonderful? Thank God for the ability to forget. Likewise Caleb urged his people, "Don't return to Egypt, don't go back, don't look back. Forget the things that are behind."

I hear people say today, "Oh, I would love to go back to the good old days." An old boy who was talking to me just the other day said exactly that—"I'd love to go back to the good old days." I don't know about you, but I don't remember any *good* old days. I began my ministry during the Depression. In fact, it came while I was still in seminary. I don't want to go back to the good old days. They weren't good, they were very bad. This is the greatest time to live—right now. I wouldn't exchange places with anybody in the past. My beloved, forget the things that are behind.

I have had several calls recently from folk who said they were contemplating suicide. This past week a girl who could barely talk for weeping said, "Pray for me. For God's sake, pray for me. I'm going to take my life." I said, "Look, if you could solve your problems by doing that, it would be all right, but you won't solve your problems. Whatever it is that is so terrible that's looming up out of the past, the Lord Jesus has already paid the penalty for your sin. Now trust Him and forget it, forget it." That's what our loving Lord has done with those things in our lives.

Oh, how many of us are overcome and overwhelmed by some failure of the past that looks around every corner and mocks us. We are hindered and thwarted and convicted and defeated today because we won't forget the past. So many are tortured with that old refrain, "It might have been, it might have been." I talked the other day to a man who said, "Oh, if I had only done differently, if I had only done differently." Well, you didn't, brother, so forget those things that are behind.

If we confess our sins, He is faithful and just to forgive us our sins and to cleanse us from all unrighteousness.
(1 John 1:9)

When I was pastor in Cleburne, Texas, a man drove up in front of my home, a man who attended the church. He was not a member. He said, "I want you to know that I am a Christian. I have not joined the church. I have not made an open confession of my faith in Christ. And the reason is that when I came to this country years ago as a young man, I killed another young man. That has always stood in my way. I've never done anything for God. But I had to kill him. It was either him or me. I have wished many times I had let him kill me."

"Well," I said, "regardless of the past, you can't go back and undo it. The thing for you to do, if you have taken Christ as your Savior, is to forget it. Because God forgets our past!"

Now let's bring this up to date. If you have trusted Christ as your Savior yet are bothered by something in your past, God says, "I will remember their sins no more." When God says that He will forget your sins, my friend, don't you start bringing them up. He's forgotten them. And when God forgets, you can be sure of one thing—it's forgotten! He says, "As far as the east is from the west, so far has He removed our transgressions from us" (Psalm 103:12). He has put them in the bottom of the ocean! Now don't dredge them up.

Have you come to Christ? Have you accepted Him as your Savior? Forget the past.

I want to turn to a statement Paul made in Colossians:

> **And you, being dead in your trespasses and the uncircumcision of your flesh, He has made alive together with Him, having forgiven you all trespasses, having wiped out the handwriting of requirements that was against us, which was contrary to us. And He has taken it out of the way, having nailed it to the cross.**
> (Colossians 2:13, 14)

Regardless of what your past might be today, regardless of your failure, all of that has been nailed to the cross, my beloved. And God has forgotten it.

In my southland, there was a Negro woman who had a radiant Christian testimony, joyful all the time. Someone asked her one day, "What is the secret of the joy of your life?" She said, "It's very simple. When I works, I works hard. When I rests, I sits loose. When I worries, I goes to sleep." The trouble with us is that when we worry we don't go to sleep.

This man Caleb forgot Egypt. He had no notion of bringing back the days of Egypt. He's going on. And, my friend, if God has forgiven you of your sins, they are in the past. Now move on!

FAITH TO FACE THE FACTS OF THE PRESENT

The second part of Caleb's formula was that he had faith to face the facts of the present. In the Book of Deuteronomy, we have a review of Israel's wilderness experiences after the Exodus and a statement from God concerning this man Caleb. Note God's provision and tender care of them through all the wilderness journey.

> "The LORD your God, who goes before you, He will fight for you, according to all He did for you in Egypt before your eyes, and in the wilderness where you saw how the LORD your God carried you, as a man carries his son, in all the way that you went until you came to this place. Yet, for all that, you did not believe the LORD your God, who went in the way before you to search out a place for you to pitch your tents, to show you the way you should go, in the fire by night and in the cloud by day."
> (Deuteronomy 1:30–33)

Notice God's promise to Caleb:

> "And the LORD heard the sound of your words, and was angry, and took an oath, saying, 'Surely not one of these men of this evil generation shall see that good land of which I swore to give to your fathers, except Caleb the son of Jephunneh; he shall see it, and to him and his children I am

**giving the land on which he walked, be-
cause he wholly followed the LORD.'"**
(Deuteronomy 1:34–36)

Caleb wholly followed the Lord! The world today is
looking for a way of escape from the facts of life. The
world is forging some little escape mechanism. A great
many people are afraid to face reality, the reality of life.
I offer no excuse for the drunkard, but right now in
Southern California thousands of people are crawling
up on a bar stool for only one reason, and that is to get
something that will deaden the pain of the reality of life.
How many today are alcoholics, not because they love
the stuff—they may hate it! But they have lapsed because they can't face life. Even many Christians are like
that, unable to face the harsh reality of life.

Vic and I were in school together as young men, and
when I was in Memphis several years ago I saw him
again. His aunt had written to me that he had become
an alcoholic. He came to the service the first night I was
speaking there, and I told him, "Vic, I'd like to talk with
you."

"Okay. Where are you staying?" And I told him the
hotel. He said, "I'll come around tomorrow."

The next morning at seven o'clock—I wasn't even out
of bed—the phone rang. He said, "Hi!"

"Well, where are you?"

"I'm downstairs."

"Fine, have breakfast with me, but I'm not even
dressed. Come on up."

He came up and I began to talk with him. First we
talked about old times. Then he wanted to tell his story

about how liquor had gotten him, and I said, "I didn't know in the old days before I was saved that you liked that stuff."

"I don't like it. Don't you remember, I was a timid-type fellow. I sort of stuttered. I never could push my way forward. I was always in the background. I felt like I was submerged and overwhelmed. Then I started drinking beer. I found out with two bottles I became a sociable fellow and I could talk. I started using it for that reason, and it's got me now. It has wrecked my life, but I hate the stuff."

He was just not willing to face the reality of life. We got down on our knees and he cried out to God for deliverance. He told God how he hated it and was shackled by it. I am delighted to say that since then he has gotten deliverance. God has marvelously and wonderfully brought him back to Himself.

How many folk today just won't face the facts of life at all and won't deal with the reality of life. When they go to church they want a sermon that is "brief, bright, and brotherly." This is the reason the cults and non-Christian religions have become popular—they do not deal with reality. To them sin is not a reality and sickness is not a reality. And you can escape all of this by following their little system.

May I say to you, my beloved, the world is in a mess right now, looking for a way out. People are frustrated like birds beating their wings in a cage, like animals pacing up and down in a zoo, like convicts in a cell—hemmed in and thwarted. Multitudes around the world just want out.

My friend, when you and I will face the reality that

we are sinners in God's sight and that in and of our-
selves we can do nothing that pleases God; when you
and I will deal with that eternal matter of sin in our
hearts and lives, then God is prepared to deal with us
and to lift us out of the muck and the mire.

I've thought of Caleb spending those forty years in
the wilderness—forty years that killed off one genera-
tion. But they didn't kill off Caleb. He didn't even age!
I can imagine some old Israelite who had been weaned
on a dill pickle meeting Caleb one morning and whining,
"Brother Caleb, isn't this desert hot? It's unbearable out
here—this is a terrible place to be!" I think Caleb would
have answered, "Yes, it is. It's hotter this morning than
usual, and certainly this desert is a terrible place. But
I'm not going to be here forever, brother. This is tempo-
rary. And I was just thinking this morning about that
spot that I saw over yonder in the Promised Land. I'm
going there someday."

Caleb could face his present situation because he
looked beyond it. God had called Israel to go into the
land of Canaan, and Caleb believed it could be done.

FAITH TO FACE THE FUTURE

Finally, Caleb had faith to face the future. Will you
notice his tremendous statement here:

**"I was forty years old when Moses the ser-
vant of the LORD sent me from Kadesh
Barnea to spy out the land, and I brought
back word to him as it was in my heart. . . .
And now, behold, the LORD has kept me
alive, as He said, these forty-five years, ever**

**since the LORD spoke this word to Moses
while Israel wandered in the wilderness;
and now, here I am this day, eighty-five
years old. . . . Now therefore, give me this
mountain of which the LORD spoke in that
day; for you heard in that day how the
Anakim were there, and that the cities were
great and fortified. It may be that the LORD
will be with me, and I shall be able to drive
them out as the LORD said."**
(Joshua 14:7, 10, 12)

The Anakim were giants. Old Caleb picked the toughest
place, but it was the best place. You see, the giants
naturally could live in the best place. They could run
out everybody else. And Caleb said, "That's the place I
want." What a man of faith he was. All those forty years
this man was looking forward to the day when he was
going to put the giants out and take over Hebron!

Years ago in the South there was a woman, a wife and
mother with a beautiful home, who was complaining
about everything and finding fault, saying, "Oh, if I
could just get away from it all." Finally her maid said
to her, "Listen, what are you trying to get away from?
This lovely home, these beautiful children, a fine husband? What is it you are trying to get away from? No
matter where you go, you're going to have to lug yourself
along!" Today a great many people say, "If I could only
escape. . . ." My friend, you can't escape. You have to
take yourself along wherever you go.

In Caleb's day, Israel did not believe God, and their
unbelief turned into disobedience. So God turned them
back into that wilderness for thirty-eight years. Re-

member that the leaders, which included Caleb, had to accept the majority decision of the people and return with them to the wilderness. How did they cope? The people spent that entire time complaining. The record we have of that period is a book filled with tears and sorrow. It's a portrait of pain, a poem of pity, a proverb of pathos, a hymn of heartbreak, a psalm of sadness, a symphony of sorrow, a story of sifting, a tale of tears, a dirge of desolation, a tragedy of travail, an account of agony. Actually it was a book of boohoos, for they boohooed all the way through the wilderness. They complained and murmured about everything. They were not willing to face up to their own failure to walk by faith with God.

Caleb knew what suffering was. And, my friend, that desert was just as real to him as it was to any Israelite. But he was walking with God. Have you ever noticed the place that he saw when he was in that land? It was in giant country. When he got back from his assignment to search out the land, he must have said to Moses, "I have seen the most beautiful spot in that land!" The name of it is Hebron. What does Hebron mean? Communion. For forty years while the children of Israel were saying, "Oh, if we could only go back to Egypt," Caleb was saying, "Wait till the day I get to Hebron"—communion with God. Those forty years in the wilderness killed off the rest of the crowd, but they didn't do a thing to him but make him healthy. They grew old, and he stayed young. The giants in the Promised Land made the others tremble and think of themselves as grasshoppers. But Caleb thought of God. For forty years he communed with God. How wonderful to get to that place!

In the New Testament the apostle Paul not only wrote "forgetting those things which are behind," (Philippians 3:13), but also, "I have learned in whatever state I am, to be content" (Philippians 4:11). I'll be honest with you, I wish I could learn that. I remember missing a plane in Houston, Texas—I don't like to fly anyway—and before the next plane out a storm had come up. Boy, was I whining! A friend of mine came out to have a little fellowship while I was waiting. We had dinner together and I just cried on his shoulder, and when it got damp I cried on his other shoulder. I told him how terrible it was. Well, he reminded me of that verse of Scripture. I must confess it was very meaningless to me at the time, "I have learned in whatever state I am, to be content."

"Caleb, how do you like the wilderness?"

"Don't like it."

"Well, you seem to be rejoicing while the rest of them are murmuring. What's the difference?"

"I have a hope for the future. Hebron is the place I want."

What a man of faith he was. All those forty years this man was looking forward to the day when he was going to put the giants out and take over Hebron!

How many Christians today are satisfied with little victories, in fact, some with no victory at all. Have you had any victories in your life, any occasion to rejoice this past week? This man Caleb, he claimed his possession. He said, "For forty years I've been living in anticipation of Hebron. I want it." My, if there were more Christians today like that who could say, "forgetting those things which are behind and reaching forward to those things which are ahead, I press toward the goal for the prize of the upward call of God in Christ Jesus" (Philippians 3:13*b*, 14). I'm not living the Christian life aimlessly. I'm living the Christian life with purpose. There's a goal. I want to see the Savior. I want to come into His presence. I want to have communion with Him.

Joshua and Caleb had been together many years, and Joshua was the one God was directing and leading. But I have a notion Joshua went to Caleb on many occasions. Joshua would say, "Caleb, how are things coming over on your side of the camp?" And Caleb would answer, "You know, this morning I spent time in the Word. I spent time this morning in prayer. I'm having communion with God." May I say to you, Christian friend, we will not only starve to death, but we will be robbed of blessing and joy and power when we fail to have communion with our God.

Caleb had faith. He had the faith to say, "God, I want You to give me my part of that land. It is called Hebron." Yes, but Caleb, giants are there. And he'd say, "I know it. I saw them forty-five years ago. They're getting old now. I'm going to drive them out, because I haven't gotten old. I'm as strong this day as I was forty-five years ago, and I'm going in and take that land." He was as ready to take on the giants now as he was when he was a young man.

The question is, did he take it? Well, look at Joshua 15:14. There you have the answer:

Caleb drove out the three sons of Anak [giants] from there: Sheshai, Ahiman, and Talmai, the children of Anak.

He drove them out, and he got Hebron. It became his possession. God was bigger than the giants.

Caleb reminds me of Adoniram Judson, the missionary who spent six years in Burma without a convert. The board that sent him out did not sense the situation nor what a tremendous missionary they had in Judson, so they wrote him a very diplomatic letter suggesting that he should come home. They asked him what the prospects were in Burma. His reply was, "The future is as bright as the promises of God." His confidence in God was the reason he could stay in the wilderness of Burma all those years. Although he suffered a great deal and it took a long time for revival to break out, it finally did. His time was well spent.

Are you enjoying all the spiritual blessings that God has for you today? You say, "I have lots of trouble." I know that Christians have many troubles in the course of their lives. My heart goes out to them. But I always think of the testimony of a man who said his favorite Bible verse was, "It came to pass." When puzzled people asked him what he meant by that, he replied, "When I get into trouble and problems pile up, I turn to my verse and know my troubles have not come to stay; they have come to *pass*." There are a lot of things you can complain about, friend, and I do my share also, but what about your hope? What about the future? Although Caleb spent forty years in that great and terrible wilderness with a bunch of crybabies, he was enjoying all the spiritual blessings that were his.

The apostle Paul said it this way:

Brethren, I do not count myself to have apprehended; but one thing I do, forgetting those things which are behind and reach-

ing forward to those things which are ahead, I press toward the goal for the prize of the upward call of God in Christ Jesus. (Philippians 3:13, 14)

Friend, someday we will be rewarded. We will not be rewarded according to the great amount of work done for God, nor according to our prominence and popularity. The important thing will be, did we wholly follow the Lord? Oh, that God's people would learn today that the most important thing in this life is to wholly follow the Lord! Caleb, man of God that he was, took Hebron. Sure, giants were there, but he said, "That's the place I want. That's the very best spot!" Oh, that you and I might press toward the mark for the high calling of God in Christ Jesus.

Perhaps you are discouraged today and need help desperately. You need a Savior, desperately. May I say to you, turn your eyes upon this Savior, the wonderful Lord Jesus Christ and trust Him now. This is the first step, the thing He is asking each one of us to do. And then there is Caleb's formula. Use it!

Faith to forget the past
Faith to face the facts of the present
Faith to face the future

— 4 —

SAMSON

The Secret of Samson's Strength (and His Weakness)

Samson is probably the only person named in the Word of God whose life, as recorded there, could easily fit into our contemporary society. That is, he would be accepted and be a very popular hero, which would be true of no one else in the Word of God, as far as I can tell. For example, Abraham is a man who is known more than any other person who ever lived; three great religions go back to Abraham—Judaism, Islam, and Christianity. More people have heard of Abraham than of any other man who ever lived. But if he were present today, may I say to you, my friend, he would not be acceptable to this day and generation in which we live. He could not be a popular man because of the standards by which he lived.

You can say the same of any other person—even

David with all of his faults. Yet David was a man after God's own heart, a man who had a real passion for God. He could never be popular in our day and generation. But this man Samson would be a man much sought after in our day, and I trust that we can see this as we look at his life.

Actually there are three significant statements that we want to look at now. First, the secret of Samson's success; second, the secret of Samson's strength; and third, the secret of Samson's failure. Now will you follow me very carefully as we look at this man Samson, because more is given concerning him than of any other of Israel's judges.

THE SECRET OF SAMSON'S SUCCESS

Samson is the last of the judges—he could have been the greatest of the judges; but, of course, he was not. The repeated apostasy of Israel forms the setting for a time of oppression by the Philistines. The Philistines were probably the worst enemies that Israel had. This time their oppression lasted for forty years.

Again the children of Israel did evil in the sight of the LORD, and the LORD delivered them into the hand of the Philistines for forty years. Now there was a certain man from Zorah, of the family of the Danites, whose name was Manoah; and his wife was barren and had no children.
(Judges 13:1, 2)

Notice the thing that is said concerning Samson's birth in Judges 13:3, 5:

And the Angel of the LORD appeared to the woman and said to her, "Indeed now, you are barren and have borne no children, but you shall conceive and bear a son. .... And no razor shall come upon his head, for the child shall be a Nazirite to God from the womb; and he shall begin to deliver Israel out of the hand of the Philistines."

Now that is the thing which is said concerning this man Samson—he could have been John the Baptist of the Old Testament, but he was not. He doesn't even compare to John the Baptist, but in his birth there is a strange similarity. Before John the Baptist was born, the Spirit of God came upon him, even in his mother's womb. That was also true of Samson.

Never was a man born with a more glorious opportunity than Samson. He had a spiritual silver spoon in his mouth, so to speak. Everything was propitious in his life for a glorious career, and a very brilliant future was before him. Before he was born, God had marked him out and raised him up for a gigantic task, and that task was to deliver Israel. May I say that the world today, and especially our nation, needs a man of this caliber—a man raised up of God, a man who stands for God against all opposition, God's man in this hour. Samson was not that man in his day, although he could have been.

Will you notice again the condition of Israel at that time. In the first verse of chapter 13 we are told:

Again the children of Israel did evil in the sight of the LORD, and the LORD delivered them into the hand of the Philistines for forty years.

Israel needed a deliverer. And this man Samson was to be the one to deliver them out from under the oppression of the Philistines. So the angel of God appeared unto Manoah and his wife and told them they were to have a son, that this son was to be a Nazirite, and that the Holy Spirit of God would come upon him from the very beginning.

Now a Nazirite was one in Israel who took a voluntary vow. No one was required to take it. But there were many men and women in Israel who dedicated their lives to the service of God on a voluntary basis, and they took what was known as the Nazirite vow. It was a threefold vow which may sound strange to you today, but it had a very definite meaning.

The first thing was, *they were not to drink wine*. And it was not just because of the alcohol content. They were not to eat raisins, they were not to eat grapes, they were to avoid anything that came from the vine. The reason was this: The "fruit of the vine" always spoke to the nation Israel of earthly joy. It was to cheer the heart. But the Nazirite was not to find his joy in anything on this earth. He was to find his joy in the things of God.

And do not be drunk with wine, in which is dissipation; but be filled with the Spirit. (Ephesians 5:18)

Samson was a Nazirite—this man of all men! Think of his life for a moment. Although he was a man dedicated to God, who was to find his joy in the things of God, there is no record that he found his joy in the things of God ever in his life! He was always finding his pleasure in the things of this world. And he was a most unhappy man—actually, the most tragic man you find on the pages of Scripture.

There are a lot of Christians just like this today. They have been called to find their joy in the Lord. The Bible tells us that the joy of the Lord is our strength, it is our portion. And Paul gave this commandment to believers, "Rejoice in the Lord always. Again I will say, rejoice!" (Philippians 4:4). That is not just backslapping or laughing—you don't have to go around grinning like a Cheshire cat to reveal you have the joy of the Lord. It's not that type of thing. It is something that is down deep in the heart, something that is very meaningful, something that comes from the Lord by the Holy Spirit. It is a fruit of the Holy Spirit: "But the fruit of the Spirit is love, joy. . ." (Galatians 5:22). Joy is the second great side benefit that can be given to us only by our Lord. The Nazirite was to find his joy in the things of God and in God Himself. That was the first requirement of the Nazirite vow.

The second thing was, *the Nazirite was not to cut his hair*. That is strange, is it not? He was not to cut his hair or shave. Samson must have been a shaggy looking fellow, by the way. We see him depicted as a big, strong, handsome fellow. But my personal opinion is that he was a small, scrawny-looking guy.

But how in the world could a man like that be such a

ladies' man, for he was that also. He never had a haircut until Delilah gave him one. The Nazirite was not to cut his hair.

Now, what did that mean? For a woman, long hair is her glory, but for a man it is his shame. The Word of God tells us this:

> **Does not even nature itself teach you that if a man has long hair, it is a dishonor to him?**
> (1 Corinthians 11:14)

The Scripture is explicit. Long hair dishonors a man. And a Nazirite would be willing to bear the shame for God. That is the whole point of it. He was to be different. John the Baptist was a Nazirite, which is the reason he looked as he did. A razor had not touched his head or face.

Third, *the Nazirite was not to come near a dead body.* When a loved one died, he was not to go to the funeral or have anything to do with it. In other words, no natural claim could make any demand upon him whatever. He had to put God first, above his relatives and loved ones. The Lord Jesus said,

> **"If anyone comes to Me and does not hate his father and mother, wife and children, brothers and sisters, yes, and his own life also, he cannot be My disciple. And whoever does not bear his cross and come after Me cannot be My disciple."**
> (Luke 14:26, 27)

This simply means that we are not to put anything before Christ. This is something we have lost sight of in our day.

Now Samson was a Nazirite. He was God's man. And that, my friend, is the secret of his successes. He was raised up for a great purpose. As he was dedicated to God, then he would be a success—but only as he performed his God-appointed task. Note the thing that is said here in Judges 13:5, "He shall begin to deliver Israel." But he never did deliver Israel. He was never actually a success. Success and opportunity knocked at his door, but the best that could be said of this man was, "He shall begin to deliver Israel."

Samson was just a beginner—he was in the beginners' class. May I say, there are a lot of Christians today who are just like this. They make a great beginning, but they do not finish a task. Paul said to the Galatians,

> **You ran well. Who hindered you from obeying the truth?**
> (Galatians 5:7)

They started out with a bang and ended up with a fizzle. Many people begin to read the Bible but fall by the wayside. They just begin and don't go on with it. I have been a pastor for forty years, friend, and I have known lots of people who start something and never conclude it. They never finish what they are called to do.

Here is this man Samson, called of God to a great task, that of delivering Israel from the domination of the Philistines. And, my friend, he could have done it, but he did not. God said, "He shall *begin* to deliver Israel"—and that's as far as he ever got. All too many Christians are like that. Samson was that kind of man.

THE SECRET OF SAMSON'S STRENGTH

Now the next thing we want to see is the secret of Samson's strength, and this is very important. In Judges 13:25 we read,

And the Spirit of the LORD began to move upon him at Mahaneh Dan between Zorah and Eshtaol.

The secret of Samson's strength was not in his arms, although he killed a thousand Philistines at one time with them. Samson's strength was not in his back, although he carried the gates of Gaza on his back, which was a remarkable undertaking. And note this very carefully, Samson's strength was not in his hair, although he was weak when it was cut. It is merely superstition to think that because he had long hair he was strong. He was a Nazirite dedicated to God, and the hair was the badge of his vow. When he lost his badge he was weak, and he was weak because the Spirit of God had departed from him. Why? Because he had failed in his vow. He had not made good.

Now this man Samson has been depicted as a big bruiser, a fellow with bulging muscles, but was he really that? As I see it, Samson was the biggest sissy in or out of the Bible. His name means "little sun"—he was the first one to go into orbit, but he didn't do very well. He was really a weakling. No matter where you see him in the Word of God, you cannot admire him at all. For instance, he went down one time to Timnah:

Now Samson went down to Timnah, and saw a woman in Timnah of the daughters of the Philistines. So he went up and told his father and mother, saying, "I have seen a woman in Timnah of the daughters of the Philistines; now therefore, get her for me as a wife."
(Judges 14:1, 2)

What a sissy! He didn't have nerve enough to go and ask the girl to marry him. He said to Mama and Papa, "You go down and get her for me." What kind of strong man is that?

You will find that he likes to make riddles. One time when a lion came roaring against him, he killed it with his bare hands—by the power of God he killed a lion. He should not have gone back to see the carcass because contact with a carcass was a violation of the Nazirite vow. But he did go back to it some time later and found that a swarm of bees had made honey in what remained of the carcass. This gave him the best riddle of his life, and he had to give out the little riddle. He was great at that sort of thing and also at playing pranks like a schoolboy. He never did grow up. One time he took the gates of Gaza, just like a college student might, put them on his back, and carried them off about forty miles to the top of a hill! That was a prank you might play in

school, but not as a grown man called of God to deliver
Israel! He had been called to deliver Israel with his
mighty, God-given power, but all he did was to use it for
his own personal advantage. He allowed every woman
to make a fool of him—and they did! He is not a he-man.
He is not the strongest man—he's the weakest man in
the Word of God!

Sometimes in advertisements of body builders you
see some little, dried-up, anemic fellow. Then alongside
it you see the picture of the fellow after he has used the
product—oh boy, what a robust figure with bulging
muscles! Now a great many people think Samson is the
picture after using the body builder, but in my opinion
he's the fellow before using it: the little, dried-up weasel.
And that is the reason folk marveled at this man. How
can this little Milquetoast fellow be so strong? He
couldn't be. And this is the reason God today has to
make some of us very weak before He can use us. He
has to let us know and let the world know that it is "'Not
by might nor by power, but by My Spirit,' says the LORD
of hosts" (Zechariah 4:6). We are told that the Spirit of
the Lord came upon Samson, and when the Spirit of the
Lord came upon him, he was strong! That is the secret
of his strength.

The world is always looking for strong things. That
is the reason they wanted to know his strength. God
chooses the weak things.

> **But God has chosen the foolish things of the
> world to put to shame the wise, and God has
> chosen the weak things of the world to put
> to shame the things which are mighty; and**

**the base things of the world and the things
which are despised God has chosen, and the
things which are not, to bring to nothing
the things that are, that no flesh should
glory in His presence.**
(1 Corinthians 1:27–29)

Samson is an illustration of this verse. God says He
chooses the foolish, the base, the despised, and the
weak. In our day when God wants that kind of man, He
can make him strong.

Samson was a hero in his day. It is always the sign
of a decadent age when they put the emphasis on the
physical. I do not want to call names, but who are the
present-day heroes? None of our scientists, no artist,
no great preacher is a hero in America. Who are the
heroes? The baseball and football players, the wres-
tlers, the fighters, the runners. It is all physical great-
ness.

I listened the other night on TV to an interview of a
baseball player and an interview of a fighter. It was
interesting. Both of them murdered the English language. But they made it very clear that the only thing
they were interested in, as one of them said, was "the
moolah," the money! That is the hero of the hour. Samson would have made a fitting hero for this time in
which we live, for people admire strong men. Believe
me, friend, when the Spirit of God came upon Samson,
he was a strong man. The people wanted to know the
secret of his strength. But the interesting thing is that
the secret of his strength was the Spirit of the Lord who
came upon him.

THE SECRET OF SAMSON'S FAILURE

Afterward it happened that he loved a woman in the Valley of Sorek, whose name was Delilah. And the lords of the Philistines came up to her and said to her, "Entice him, and find out where his great strength lies, and by what means we may overpower him, that we may bind him to afflict him; and every one of us will give you eleven hundred pieces of silver."
(Judges 16:4, 5)

You may be sure that she was much more interested in silver than she was in Samson.

So Delilah said to Samson, "Please tell me where your great strength lies, and with what you may be bound to afflict you."
(v. 6)

He teases her at first.

And Samson said to her, "If they bind me with seven fresh bowstrings, not yet dried, then I shall become weak, and be like any other man." So the lords of the Philistines brought up to her seven fresh bowstrings, not yet dried, and she bound him with them.
(vv. 7, 8)

He allowed her to tie him up with ropes—again he is playing with her.

Now men were lying in wait, staying with her in the room. And she said to him, "The Philistines are upon you, Samson!" But he broke the bowstrings as a strand of yarn breaks when it touches fire. So the secret of his strength was not known. Then Delilah said to Samson, "Look, you have mocked me and told me lies. Now, please tell me what you may be bound with." So he said to her, "If they bind me securely with new ropes that have never been used, then I shall become weak, and be like any other man." Therefore Delilah took new ropes and bound him with them, and said to him, "The Philistines are upon you, Samson!" And men were lying in wait, staying in the room. But he broke them off his arms like a thread.
(vv. 9–12)

She is getting exasperated with her boyfriend.

Delilah said to Samson, "Until now you have mocked me and told me lies. Tell me what you may be bound with." And he said to her, "If you weave the seven locks of my head into the web of the loom"—So she wove it tightly with the batten of the loom, and said to him, "The Philistines are upon you, Samson!" But he awoke from his sleep, and pulled out the batten and the web from the loom. Then she said to him, "How can you say, 'I love you,' when your heart is not with me? You have mocked me these three

**times, and have not told me where your
great strength lies." And it came to pass,
when she pestered him daily with her
words and pressed him, so that his soul was
vexed to death, that he told her all his heart,
and said to her, "No razor has ever come
upon my head, for I have been a Nazirite to
God from my mother's womb. If I am
shaven, then my strength will leave me, and
I shall become weak, and be like any other
man."**
(vv. 13–17)

One of the greatest sins that destroys many men today
is this matter of illicit sex. That was Samson's sin. As
far as we know, he made no attempt to marry Delilah.

**When Delilah saw that he had told her all
his heart, she sent and called for the lords
of the Philistines, saying, "Come up once
more, for he has told me all his heart." So
the lords of the Philistines came up to her
and brought the money in their hand. Then
she lulled him to sleep on her knees, and
called for a man and had him shave off the
seven locks of his head. Then she began to
torment him, and his strength left him. And
she said, "The Philistines are upon you,
Samson!" So he awoke from his sleep, and
said, "I will go out as before, at other times,
and shake myself free!" But he did not know
that the LORD had departed from him. Then
the Philistines took him and put out his
eyes, and brought him down to Gaza. They**

**bound him with bronze fetters, and he be-
came a grinder in the prison.**
(vv. 18–21)

I think this is one of the most tragic statements you
will find in the Bible. Certainly it is the most tragic
statement made about Samson. You see, every time this
man wanted to move, the Spirit of God came upon him.
But he kept playing, he kept trifling. One day he went
out, thinking the Spirit of God would move through him
again, but "he did not know that the LORD had departed
from him." How tragic it is. That is the failure in his life.

Now again notice very carefully what it says in verse
4 concerning Delilah, "Afterward it happened that he
loved a woman"—illicit love. That was the undoing of
Samson, and that is the story of his life. He loved a
woman. No man falls suddenly. No man has ever fallen
suddenly. It is always gradual.

Go back and look at this man's story. He began that
same way. He goes down to the Philistine country. He
should have gone down to deliver his people from the
relentless Philistine oppression, but instead of delivering, he sees a Philistine woman in Timnah. He comes
back and says to Papa and Mama, "I want you to get her
for me." They say, "Why don't you marry one of the
Hebrew women? Why go down and get a Philistine, an
enemy?" He says, "I want her, I like her. Go get her for
me."

So they go down—he's a pampered boy—and they get
her for him. Well, he didn't keep her long because he's
always playing tricks. Oh, he had a good one there in
Timnah. We won't go into the details now but, my, he

really played some tricks there with the Philistines. He would have his fun. After the Philistines made him angry, he caught three hundred foxes, tied some firebrands to the tails of those foxes (isn't that *fun!*), and turned them loose in the wheat fields of the Philistines. He never did deliver Israel. He never caused people to rally to him, he never raised an army, he never did anything significant. He loved a woman. That was his weakness, that was his downfall.

May I say to you, we are living in the times of which Dr. Pitirim Sirokin, a sociologist at Harvard University, made this statement:

> If more and more individuals are brought up in this sex-saturated atmosphere then, without deep and moral restraint, they will become rudderless folk controlled only by the wind of their environment.

I have been reading a very fine book on this particular subject. Why is it that in our day we are seeing so much divorce—when we have books on marriage, seminars on marriage, marriage counselors, and marriage psychologists ad infinitum? I think it goes back to the fact that there is such a great emphasis on sex. This stimuli has been given such tremendous emphasis that two young people do not have a chance to really fall in love. They do not have a chance to respect each other and to admire each other.

Any boy, when he is sixteen, seventeen, or eighteen years old, wants to worship a girl. But today they soon go too far, and as a result, the girl hates herself. Of course she does. She has to, especially if she has had any kind of Christian upbringing. And the boy will despise himself. As a result, if they marry on such a low plane, there is not that real love which binds them together. Oh, Samson knew a great deal about sex. But he knew nothing about marital love. He sure would make a hit today!

May I say to you, this man made a fool of himself with Delilah—or I should say that she made a fool of him. This was bound to happen, as it is bound to happen to any man with a similar attitude. Whatever his weakness is, it will eventually be the thing that will destroy him. And there came the day when Samson saw Delilah—and she was really a match for him, the only woman he ever met who was a match for him. He fell in love with her.

Delilah was a woman of the Philistines. The lords of the Philistines came to her and in substance they said, "We want to get at this man, and you're our way of doing it. We've got to find out the secret of his strength. We know it's not his muscles—it's not physical strength. We know that he is being given a strength that is not his own, and we need to know the secret of it." And they offered a handsome reward:

"Entice him, and find out where his great strength lies, and by what means we may overpower him, that we may bind him to afflict him; and every one of us will give you eleven hundred pieces of silver."
(Judges 16:5)

So she began to work on Samson. And you know

Samson—he is always going to play. One time he said, "If you will tie me with some brand new rope, then you'll get me." He wanted to have his fun. So she tied him up and then she said, "Samson, the Philistines are upon you!" Oh, how much fun he had when he broke the ropes and watched the Philistines run for the tall timber!

Then Delilah came to Samson and began to pout. She said, "You don't love me. If you loved me, you would tell me." And she kept asking him, and he tricked her again, but the third time we see him weakening. He said, "If you weave the seven locks of my head into the web of the loom"—he is getting close now. Finally, after this third attempt, and he had deceived her all three times—

> **Then she said to him, "How can you say, 'I love you,' when your heart is not with me? You have mocked me these three times, and have not told me where your great strength lies." And it came to pass, when she pestered him daily with her words and pressed him, so that his soul was vexed to death, that he told her all his heart, and said to her, "No razor has ever come upon my head, for I have been a Nazirite to God from my mother's womb. If I am shaven, then my strength will leave me, and I shall become weak, and be like any other man."**
> (vv. 15–17)

Now she sees what a fool he really is—and he was a fool.

When Delilah saw that he had told her all

his heart, she sent and called for the lords
of the Philistines, saying, "Come up once
more, for he has told me all his heart." So
the lords of the Philistines came up to her
and brought the money in their hand. Then
she lulled him to sleep on her knees, and
called for a man and had him shave off the
seven locks of his head. Then she began to
torment him, and his strength left him. And
she said, "The Philistines are upon you,
Samson!"
(vv. 18–20*a*)

This is the tragic time in the life of Samson:

So he awoke from his sleep, and said, "I will
go out as before, at other times, and shake
myself free!" But he did not know that the
LORD had departed from him.
(v. 20*b*)

Now, my beloved, when Samson lost his hair, that was
not the reason he was weak. The fact of his weakness is
this: he says, "I will go out as before, at other times, and
shake myself free!" That was all he had ever had to do.
But this time, "he did not know that the LORD had
departed from him." That was the thing that made him
weak. May I say to you, this man kidded with Delilah at
first, and played, and finally he opened up his heart like
a fool. It was Kipling who described it thus:

A fool there was and he made his prayer
   (Even as you and I!)

To a rag and a bone and a hank of hair
  (We called her the woman who did not care)
But the fool he called her his lady fair—
  (Even as you and I!)

"The Vampire" Stanza I

That was Delilah. And that was Samson, if you please. That is their story. She never knew much about love, and he didn't know much about it either. They didn't really love each other. They knew a great deal about sex, but nothing about love. He deceived her, and she betrayed him.

Then the Philistines took him and put out his eyes, and brought him down to Gaza. They bound him with bronze fetters, and he became a grinder in the prison.
(Judges 16:21)

Now he's weak as any other man, and blind, and doing the work of a beast of burden in the prison of the enemy.

I think that Samson, and another man who fell the same way, Solomon, are the two most tragic men in the entire Word of God. No two men ever had the opportunities they had. Think of it, my beloved, this man Samson was called to deliver Israel, but he was a carnal judge. He had a moral weakness. He never raised an army, he never rallied his people around him, finally he was captured, his eyes were blinded, and he became a helpless prisoner of the enemy because the Spirit of God had departed from him.

However, the hair of his head began to grow

again after it had been shaven. Now the lords of the Philistines gathered together to offer a great sacrifice to Dagon their god, and to rejoice. And they said:

"Our god has delivered into our hands Samson our enemy!"

When the people saw him, they praised their god; for they said:

"Our god has delivered into our hands our enemy,
The destroyer of our land,
And the one who multiplied our dead."

So it happened, when their hearts were merry, that they said, "Call for Samson, that he may perform for us." So they called for Samson from the prison, and he performed for them. And they stationed him between the pillars. Then Samson said to the lad who held him by the hand, "Let me feel the pillars which support the temple, so that I can lean on them." Now the temple was full of men and women. All the lords of the Philistines were there—about three thousand men and women on the roof watching while Samson performed.

Then Samson called to the LORD, saying, "O Lord GOD, remember me, I pray! Strengthen me, I pray, just this once, O God, that I may with one blow take vengeance on the Phil-

istines for my two eyes!" And Samson took
hold of the two middle pillars which sup-
ported the temple, and he braced himself
against them, one on his right and the other
on his left. Then Samson said, "Let me die
with the Philistines!" And he pushed with
all his might, and the temple fell on the
lords and all the people who were in it. So
the dead that he killed at his death were
more than he had killed in his life. And his
brothers and all his father's household
came down and took him, and brought him
up and buried him between Zorah and Eshtaol in the tomb of his father Manoah. He
had judged Israel twenty years.
(Judges 16:22–31)

Now, may I conclude like this: There is an interesting
comparison to be made of Samson to our Lord. The birth
of each of them was foretold by an angel. Both of them
were separated to God from the womb. Both of them
were Nazirites. Jesus Christ was a Nazirite in the true
sense of the word—that is, wholly devoted to God. They
were not to put anything ahead of God. Both of them
moved in the power of the Holy Spirit. Both of them were
rejected by their people. Both of them destroyed (or will
destroy) their enemies by their death. But may I say
that the comparison ends there. From there on it is a
contrast. "The ruler of this world is coming," our Lord said,
"and he has [finds] nothing in Me" (John 14:30*b*). He found
something in Samson. Samson lived a life of sin; Jesus'
life was sinless. Christ on the cross prayed, "Father,
forgive them, for they do not know what they do" (Luke

23:34). Samson prayed, when he stretched out his arms on the pillars in the Temple of Dagon, "O God, that I may with one blow take vengeance on the Philistines for my two eyes!" (Judges 16:28). In death, Christ's arms were outstretched in love. In death, the arms of Samson were outstretched in anger. Samson died; Christ lives.

Somebody says, "But the day of Samson is gone and we are living in a different era." Yes, that is true. In Old Testament times the Spirit of God came upon men to accomplish a specific work, then He left them. That is not true today. David could pray at the time of his sin, "Do not take Your Holy Spirit from me" (Psalm 51:11). No Christian will ever have to pray that. The minute you are regenerated by the Holy Spirit, you are sealed by the Holy Spirit. But you and I can grieve and quench the Holy Spirit until He absolutely becomes inoperative in our lives. I am confident today that there are many Christians who have played and toyed with sin so long that never again will the Spirit of God use them.

I talked to a minister not long ago who is in his fifties. He said, "God is through with me." You bet He is. He told me his story. He said, "God is through with me, and there is a sin unto death." And that is true according to the Scripture in 1 John 5:16. You can so play and toy with sin, my beloved, until the Spirit of God is no longer operative in your life; although He won't leave you, if you have been truly born again, you can reach that place.

There is a message here for an unsaved person also. You can hear the good news of salvation by faith in Christ and you can trifle with it until there comes that fateful day when it's too late. Oh, God's mercy is always extended. But you yourself can reach the place, psychologically, when you can no longer make a decision for Christ. I talked to a man in a cult who said to me on his deathbed, "I have so toyed with sin that although I know you are presenting the true way of salvation to me, I cannot truthfully, honestly, and sincerely believe. When I say I believe, I don't know whether I do or not."

Oh, my friends, you can keep playing with the Spirit of God until the day comes when you will be hard as nails—never, never able to turn to Him. Or, if you are a believer, God will withdraw His power—not His presence—and may even take you home.

Don't trifle with God. If you have never trusted Him, do it now. If you are a Christian, confess your sin and forsake it.

— 5 —

TAMAR, RAHAB, RUTH, BATHSHEBA:

Stepping-Stones of Salvation

Not many people find the genealogies of Scripture interesting. In fact, they find them boring, monotonous. Yet a closer look at these long lists of names can turn up buried treasure, because each name has a story to tell us, if we are willing to dig a little.

When I was a young person attending a young people's conference, the Bible teacher asked the question, "How many of you young people have read through the Bible during the past year?" Not a hand went up. After some prodding, a young fellow put up his hand rather gingerly. The teacher asked, "Have you read through the Bible this past year?" "Well," he said, "I read everything except the 'begots,' and I just passed over them because they were meaningless to me." The group laughed, and the Bible teacher said, "That's what I do also. I pass over them."

From that moment down to the present, the "begots" of the Bible have interested me a great deal. Let me quote a few verses:

The book of the genealogy of Jesus Christ, the Son of David, the Son of Abraham: Abraham begot Isaac, Isaac begot Jacob, and Jacob begot Judah and his brothers. Judah begot Perez and Zerah by Tamar, Perez begot Hezron, and Hezron begot Ram. Ram begot Amminadab, Amminadab begot Nahshon, and Nahshon begot Salmon. Salmon begot Boaz by Rahab, Boaz begot Obed by Ruth, Obed begot Jesse, and Jesse begot David the king. David the king begot Solomon by her who had been the wife of Uriah.
(Matthew 1:1–6)

On the surface, you could not find anything more boring than that. But I have come to the firm conviction that the *begots* are one of the most important parts of the Word of God! You can define the Old Testament like this: It is the family history of Jesus Christ. Therefore, the genealogies in the Old Testament, beginning with Adam and moving right on through into the New Testament, come to Jesus Christ. The New Testament opens with this genealogy.

Now unfortunately, when it comes to giving out New Testaments, I have always felt that there should also be a word of caution given, especially to those reading it for the first time. A chaplain once told me, "In World War II, I gave out literally thousands of New Testaments. I have handed them out to boys who had never even seen a Bible before, sometimes in the bunks and sometimes on the front line. As soon as the boys got hold of those Bibles, they would open them up and start reading. But they didn't read long. They would just bog down with all those long names." So they never made it past this genealogy in Matthew, chapter one. It is boring, yet it is probably the most important part of the New Testament, for the New Testament stands or falls on the accuracy of this genealogy.

Obviously, the genealogies were kept in the temple, and when Titus, the Roman general, destroyed the temple in A.D. 70, the genealogies were lost. However, when Jesus was making His claim, the genealogies were still there. It is very interesting to note that, though the enemies of Jesus questioned everything else, they never questioned His genealogy. The reason is obvious—the genealogies proved that the Lord Jesus was who He claimed to be as far as His ancestry was concerned. He is the son of David, and He is also the son of Abraham, for He came in that line which God said would produce the Messiah.

Notice that Matthew begins his Gospel by declaring this fact:

The book of the genealogy of Jesus Christ, the Son of David, the Son of Abraham.
(Matthew 1:1)

A careful reading of the genealogy that follows is

more than interesting; it is thrilling. Four names stand out as if they were neon lights. It is startling to find them included in the genealogy of Christ. First, they are the names of women; second, they are the names of Gentiles!

Women did not get into genealogies—but don't find fault with the people of that day, because today we do the same thing in marriage. The name that the couple takes is the name of the man. They don't take the name of the woman. Her line ends; his goes on. That's the way we do it today, and that's the way they did it back then.

Down through the years, I have performed weddings where the girl had a lovely name like Jones or Smith, and she wanted to exchange it for a name like Neuenschwander or Schicklegruber! You would think that she would not want to surrender her name for one having four or five syllables, but that's the way we do it today. In my files I have a clipping from some years ago that tells of a couple in Pasadena who did the unusual thing of taking the name of the woman, which, I understand, can be done legally. But our custom is for the woman to take the name of her husband, and it is the man's genealogy that is given.

In Jesus' day it was indeed unusual to find in a genealogy a woman's name, yet here in the Bible we have four names. Again, these are not only four women, they are four Gentiles. As you may know, God in the Mosaic Law said that His people were not to intermarry with tribes that were heathen and pagan. Even Abraham was instructed by God to send back to his own people to get a bride for his son Isaac. Also, the same thing was done by Isaac for his son Jacob. It was God's arrangement that monotheism, worship of one true God, should be the prevailing belief of those who were in the line leading down to the Lord Jesus Christ. Yet in His genealogy are the names of four gentile women. Two of them were Canaanites, one was a Moabite, and the fourth was a Hittite! You would naturally ask the question, "How did *they* get into the genealogy of Christ?"

Upon examination we find that, even in the genealogy of Christ, God has woven in the story of salvation. In fact, we have the stepping-stones of salvation in the genealogy of Christ.

The New Testament opens with these words: "The book of the geneology [or generation] of Jesus Christ. . . . " That is an unusual expression. If you would begin at Matthew 1:2 and go all the way through the New Testament to the end of Revelation, you would not again find the expression, "the book of the generation of" anybody. This is the only place it occurs—it opens the New Testament. You may say, "Then it must be found many times back in the Old Testament, since that gives the family line that leads to Christ." But you can begin with Malachi and thumb your way back through the prophetic books, the poetic books, the historical section to the Pentateuch, and you still won't find it. You can go through Deuteronomy, Numbers, Leviticus, Exodus, right on back to Genesis; and when you get to the sixth chapter of Genesis, you'll say, "It looks like it's not here." But in the fifth chapter you begin reading, "This is the book of the genealogy of Adam." And that is the only other place it occurs in the Bible.

So we know that there are two books: the book of the
generations of Adam and the book of the generations of
Jesus Christ. The book of Adam is the book of death. All
of us are in that book. "In Adam all die. . . . " (1 Corinthians 15:22). If the Rapture does not occur first, all of
us will die.

> **Therefore, just as through one man sin en-
> tered the world, and death through sin, and
> thus death spread to all men, because all
> sinned.**
> (Romans 5:12)

We belong to the family of Adam, every one of us. And
in the family of Adam we are all related because of the
fact that death has "spread to" all of us. That is the book
of death, and we are all written in it.

There is another book. It is the book of the generation
of the Lord Jesus Christ. It is the Lamb's Book of Life. The
Book of Life is opposite from the book of death, but you
get into it the same way you get into the first book. You
get into Adam's book by being born into the family of
Adam. You get into the Lamb's Book of Life by the new
birth, by being born into God's family. That is the reason
our Lord said to Nicodemus that he must be born again:

> **"Most assuredly, I say to you, unless one is
> born again, he cannot see the kingdom of
> God."**
> (John 3:3)

You get into the Book of Life by faith in the Lord Jesus
Christ:

By as many as received Him, to them He gave the right to become children of God, to those who believe in His name.
(John 1:12)

Let's look at some of the individuals in the Lamb's Book of Life and the story of salvation that is woven into the genealogy found in the Gospel of Matthew. I want to lift out the names of the four gentile women and see how they got into the genealogy of Christ.

TAMAR—SIN

The first name occurs in Matthew 1:3, "Judah begot Perez and Zerah by Tamar. . . . "

You cannot read her story in Genesis 38 without coming to the conclusion that this woman got into the genealogy of Christ for just one reason—she was a sinner. If she had not been a sinner, she would not have gotten into the genealogy of Christ.

You see, Tamar had married two of the sons of Judah, and the Lord had destroyed them both because of their wickedness. Judah then promised her his third son, Shelah, when he was old enough to marry. But he did not keep his word, so Tamar took matters into her own hands:

Now in the process of time the daughter of Shua, Judah's wife, died; and Judah was comforted, and went up to his sheep-shearers at Timnah, he and his friend Hirah the Adullamite. And it was told Tamar, saying, "Look, your father-in-law is going

up to Timnah to shear his sheep." So she took off her widow's garments, covered herself with a veil and wrapped herself, and sat in an open place which was on the way to Timnah; for she saw that Shelah was grown, and she was not given to him as a wife. When Judah saw her, he thought she was a harlot, because she had covered her face. Then he turned to her by the way, and said, "Please let me come in to you"; for he did not know that she was his daughter-in-law. So she said, "What will you give me, that you may come in to me?" And he said, "I will send a young goat from the flock." So she said, "Will you give me a pledge till you send it?" Then he said, "What pledge shall I give you?" So she said, "Your signet and cord, and your staff that is in your hand." Then he gave them to her, and went in to her, and she conceived by him.
(Genesis 38:12–18)

She tricked her father-in-law and was clever enough to get proof that he was the father of her child:

And it came to pass, about three months after, that Judah was told, saying, "Tamar your daughter-in-law has played the harlot; furthermore she is with child by harlotry." So Judah said, "Bring her out and let her be burned!" When she was brought out, she sent to her father-in-law, saying, "By the man to whom these belong, I am with child." And she said, "Please determine

whose these are—the signet and cord, and staff." So Judah acknowledged them and said, "She has been more righteous than I, because I did not give her to Shelah my son." And he never knew her again.
(Genesis 38:24–26)

Tamar was a sinner and she got into Christ's genealogy on that basis.

And do you know that God starts with all of us on the basis that we are sinners? The Lord Jesus said, "I have not come to call the righteous, but sinners, to repentance" (Luke 5:32). The reason He said this is that there were no righteous. The whole human family comes under one category—sinners.

You and I begin with Him there. We have nothing to offer God. I do not know where the notion has come from that when God gets us He really gets something worthwhile and that we have something to offer God. He is in the business of saving *sinners*—no one else. And if you haven't come to Him as a sinner, you have not come to Him, because you haven't come to the only meeting place. God begins with us where we are and with what we are and how we are. And He says to us, "All have sinned and fall short of the glory of God" (Romans 3:23). There is a revolution going on today in the moral realm and in the social realm as this present generation attaches its new values to society. Isaiah the prophet said that the day would come when the world would call good evil and evil good, and that day has come. Today evil is spoken of as being good, and good is spoken of as being evil.

For example, I am amazed that out in the Hawaiian Islands the whole pitch to the tourist is that the Hawaiians were living wonderful, happy pagan lives, and those mean old missionaries came out and put them under Christianity, which has been a terrible thing. May I say to you, nothing could be further from the truth. Anyone who will look at an accurate history of the Hawaiian Islands will know that the first white men who went there were the traders, and they robbed the Hawaiians and gave them venereal disease. As a result, the Hawaiians had sunk as low as people could sink, morally. Then the missionaries came, and a revival broke out. And, my beloved, the Hawaiian people were lifted out of their fear and depression, and they became a truly joyful people.

In a day that calls good evil and evil good, a social revolution is going on. But men in the past—even in the pagan world—have recognized that this thing that the Bible calls sin is a reality. Seneca, the Roman philosopher, said: "We must say of ourselves that we are evil, have been evil, and unhappily I must add, shall be also in the future. Nobody can deliver himself. Someone must stretch out a hand to lift him up." That's from a pagan philosopher, outside of the influence of the Word of God.

Now, I won't debate the point that there are different levels of sinners. But we are all under sin. Men in jail are there for different crimes. Some are there for that which may not be very serious; others are there for serious crimes. But they all have this one thing in common: They are all in jail. And you, wherever you are, may not feel that you are a great sinner. You may be a respectable sinner. You may be a sinner who is held in high estimation in the community. But do you know why? It is only because the common grace of God has been extended to you. It is only by the grace of God that you are not down in the gutter.

You and I have the same nature that has put men in penitentiaries, that has sent some to a drunken grave, and has caused others to commit murder. You and I have that nature. But why haven't we done such things? The reason we haven't is because of the common grace of God. God begins with us where we are.

Our Lord called Zacchaeus to come down out of that tree because the man was a publican and a sinner. Jesus said, "Zacchaeus, make haste and come down, for today I must stay at your house" (Luke 19:5). Why did He not go to the mayor or to the so-called good people of the town? He called on this publican in order to let the world know that He had come to call *sinners*.

The classic example is found in the Book of Exodus when God came down to deliver His people Israel out of Egyptian bondage. God told Moses that He had come to deliver them for two reasons. God did not say, "I'm coming down to deliver them because they love Me, and they are serving Me, and they have been faithful to Me." Nor did He say, "They are righteous people and have not indulged in sin. I like them and I've come down to save them." These were not the reasons God gave Moses, because none of those things were true.

The children of Israel had gone into idolatry. They were so steeped in idolatry that when they got into the wilderness they couldn't wait to make a golden calf and fall down and worship it. They were idolaters. Were they righteous? After forty years in the wilderness, God said through Moses:

> **"Therefore understand that the LORD your God is not giving you this good land to possess because of your righteousness, for you are a stiff-necked people."**
> (Deuteronomy 9:6)

Well, then, what was it in these people that would appeal to God? Listen to Him:

> **And the LORD said: "I have surely seen the oppression of My people who are in Egypt, and have heard their cry because of their taskmasters, for I know their sorrows."**
> (Exodus 3:7)

That's all. He heard their cry. They were down there in slavery. The taskmasters' lashes had been on their backs, and in those long, weary days and nights they cried out for deliverance. God says, "I heard them."

My friend, if there is a sinner anywhere who has a need and will cry out to God, He will deliver that person:

> **So God heard their groaning, and God remembered His covenant with Abraham, with Isaac, and with Jacob.**
> (Exodus 2:24)

God had made a covenant with Abraham, even giving him details of the Egyptian captivity:

> **Then He said to Abram: "Know certainly that your descendants will be strangers in a land that is not theirs, and will serve them, and they will afflict them four hundred years. And also the nation whom they serve I will judge; afterward they shall come out with great possessions.**
> (Genesis 15:13, 14)

You see, God had predicted the Egyptian captivity and had promised to deliver them. He made good His covenant.

Anselm, that great twelfth-century saint of God, wrote on the subject of redemption using strong language: "I would rather go to hell without sin, than go to heaven with sin." And I wish that truth could get through to folk today. Do you think that you can go to heaven just as you are? Do you think that you can enter heaven with sin in your life? My friend, that sin must be dealt with. A holy God today says that He cannot receive us until a change has been wrought in our lives.

It was Alexander MacClaren, the great Scottish preacher, who said,

> It is not because God is great and I am small. It is not because He lives forever and my life is but a handbreadth. It is not because of the difference between His omniscience and my ignorance, His strength and my weakness, that I am parted from Him. "Your sins have separated between you and your God." [*That's the language of Scripture.*] And no man, build he Babels ever so high, can reach thither. There is one means by which the separation is at an end, and by which all objective hin-

drances to union and all subjective hindrances are
alike swept away. Christ has come, and in Him the
heavens have bended down to touch, and touching
to bless this low earth. And man and God are at
one once more.

Christ, my friend, can bring a sinner to God. He alone
can do that. But you'll have to begin with Him—at His
place, at His time, on His terms. And He says you are a
sinner. That's where He begins.

Long before I appeared in this world, way back yonder
in eternity, God the Father and God the Son made a
covenant. In effect, the Father said, "That fellow Vernon
McGee, he's going to be a sinner and he will need a Savior.
He will be lost unless I provide a salvation for him."

The Son said, "I love him. I'll go and die for him and
pay his penalty."

The Father said, "I love him. And I'll save him if he
will trust Me." God made a covenant that He would save
every sinner who would trust the Lord Jesus' substitu-
tionary death. God will break His Word if He does not
save you. God said, "I remembered my covenant with
Abraham, Isaac, and Jacob, and I am come down to
deliver them."

My beloved, God does not save us because He finds
anything worthwhile in us. In fact, over in the third
chapter of Romans we read:

**For all have sinned and fall short of the
glory of God, being justified freely by His
grace through the redemption that is in
Christ Jesus.**
(Romans 3:23, 24)

That word *freely* means "without a cause." It is the Greek word *dorean*, the same word the Lord Jesus used when He said, "They hated Me without a cause." We are justified without a cause. That is, when God saves us, He does not find explanation in us at all. The only thing in us that appeals to Him is our lost condition.

> *Your best resolutions must wholly be waived,*
> *Your highest ambitions be crossed;*
> *You never need think you will ever be saved,*
> *Until you've learned you are lost.*
>
> Author Unknown

God begins with you as a lost soul. He begins with you as a sinner. If you haven't come that route, you have not come. My friend, you have to begin there.

Tamar got into the genealogy of Christ because of her sin.

RAHAB—FAITH

The second name that stands out in neon lights is Rahab. "Salmon begot Boaz by Rahab. . . . " (Matthew 1:5).

Rahab! That's a name to marvel at—she was a Gentile, a Canaanite, and a prostitute!

By faith the harlot Rahab did not perish with those who did not believe, when she had received the spies with peace.
(Hebrews 11:31)

She got into the genealogy of Christ by faith. I suppose

there is no one who would contend that Rahab got into the genealogy of Christ because of her character, because of who she was. She got into the genealogy of Christ because of faith.

When the spies came into the city of Jericho, the testimony of this woman was remarkable. Listen to her as she speaks now to the spies:

"I know that the LORD has given you the land, that the terror of you has fallen on us, and that all the inhabitants of the land are fainthearted because of you. For we have heard how the LORD dried up the water of the Red Sea for you when you came out of Egypt, and what you did to the two kings of the Amorites who were on the other side of the Jordan, Sihon and Og, whom you utterly destroyed."
(Joshua 2:9, 10)

"Rahab, what was that you heard?"

"I heard how the Lord dried up the water of the Red Sea for you."

"That was forty years ago—and you heard about it? Do you mean that the city of Jericho knew about this?"

"Yes."

If you think God was a little hasty in destroying the inhabitants of Jericho, consider the fact that He had given them forty years. How much longer did you want Him to give them? In fact, the people of Israel marked time in the wilderness until the iniquity of these people was full. God was giving them an opportunity to turn to Him, and they had forty years to do it! The same God is patient with our nation today, and this has a lot of people fooled. They think He is not going to do anything because He is patiently waiting in the background. He is long-suffering and He is merciful, not willing that any should perish. God does not like to judge—judgment is His strange work. He wants to save.

Let me ask a question: Would God have saved the mayor of Jericho and the city council if they had turned to Him? Would God have saved the average citizen in Jericho? My friend, since He saved Rahab the harlot, He would have saved anybody who would have turned to Him. "By faith the harlot Rahab did not perish with those who did not believe." They had opportunity to believe but did not. This woman believed, and God saved her.

"And as soon as we heard these things, our hearts melted; neither did there remain any more courage in anyone because of you, for the LORD your God, He is God in heaven above and on earth beneath. Now therefore, I beg you, swear to me by the LORD, since I have shown you kindness, that you also will show kindness to my father's house, and give me a true token. (Joshua 2:11, 12)

Here is a remarkable woman. I'll go along with anyone who wants to say that she is the worst person in the city of Jericho—but look at her faith! When word came to her people forty years before, they were afraid, but they did nothing about it. Years went by, and when this woman was told as a child, "There are people coming through the wilderness who say God has given to them our land," in her heart she believed God. And by faith God saved her.

Let me pass on some definitions of faith. "Real faith is not that which a man holds, but that which holds him. Real faith is not that which a man assents to, but that which he submits to." There are a great many people today who only nod their heads and say, "Yes, I'm a Christian." My friend, that is not saving faith. Saving faith is when you believe God and you submit to Him. "Real faith is not an object of worship, but an impulse of life." Spurgeon said, "It is not thy joy in Christ that saves thee; it is Christ. It is not even thy faith in Christ, though that be the instrument; it is Christ's blood and merit."

Not by works of righteousness which we have done, but according to His mercy He saved us, through the washing of regeneration and renewing of the Holy Spirit.
(Titus 3:5)

Yet down through the ages, the skeptic's scorn has followed after the preaching of God's Word. In 1948 Dr. W. T. Stace, a professor of philosophy at Princeton University, wrote this in an article for the October issue of *Atlantic Monthly*:

For my part, I believe in no religion at all. With the disappearance of God from the sky, all this has changed. Since the world is not ruled by a spiritual being, but rather by blind forces, there cannot be any ideals, moral or otherwise. We live in a dead universe and there's no friend in the sky.

May I say, he would have made a good citizen of Jericho. They did not believe either.

Put that in contrast to what Martin Luther said. Someone asked Luther, "Do you feel you have been forgiven?" He answered, "No, but I'm as sure as there's a God in heaven. For feelings come and feelings go, and feelings are deceiving. My warrant is the Word of God. Naught else is worth believing." That's faith in God's Word, my beloved.

Man is justified by faith, not by works, not by character, not by anything else. The only thing we have to hold out to God is the weak hand of faith. Then He will do the rest.

Here is this woman Rahab. She had no claim on God. But she got into the genealogy of Christ because she believed God. She was saved on that basis and that alone, and we are saved on that basis alone.

RUTH—GRACE

Now we come to the third woman who is mentioned here, Ruth. "Salmon begot Boaz by Rahab, Boaz begot Obed by Ruth. . . " (Matthew 1:5).

Ruth is a Moabite, but she is a delightful person. The first two women we have considered were pretty sorry. You can't say much for Tamar and you can't say much for Rahab; but you can say a whole lot for Ruth. Actually, she is not presented on the pages of Scripture as a sinner. Have you ever noticed that? She is a woman of beauty and a woman of character.

Well, did she get in the genealogy of Christ because she was a lovely person? No. She could never have gotten into the genealogy of Christ because of her loveliness. There happened to be a law that shut her out. The Mosaic Law said:

"An Ammonite or Moabite shall not enter the assembly of the LORD; even to the tenth generation none of his descendants shall enter the assembly of the LORD forever." (Deuteronomy 23:3)

The Law condemned her. The Law always condemned the best people who have ever lived. The Law shut her out.

If you read the Book of Ruth, you will find that this was the thing her mother-in-law had told her while still in the land of Moab, before they left for Bethlehem. Naomi had called together her two daughters-in-law, Orpah and Ruth, and talked to them like a Dutch uncle talks to a redheaded stepchild. In effect, this is what she said to them:

"Don't you know if you go back with me that my people will ostracize you because you are Moabites? The Mosaic Law shuts you out. You would never be accepted among my people. You will have to take perpetual poverty, for I've lost everything. And you will have to accept perpetual widowhood, because no man among my people would risk marrying a Moabite."

Orpah said, "Well, that's all I need to hear. I'm going back to my own family."

Then Naomi said to Ruth, "Look, your sister-in-law has

gone back to her people and to her gods. You go back too."

"No," Ruth said. "I made a decision for God, and I'm willing to pay the price, whatever it is. I'm going with you." And so she went with Naomi back to Bethlehem.

One day Boaz came into the field and saw her gleaning there. It was love at first sight. Because of what her mother-in-law had said, Ruth was startled to find that someone was interested in her, and her question was:

"Why have I found favor in your eyes, that you should take notice of me, since I am a foreigner?"
(Ruth 2:10)

I can answer her question. I could say to her: *Ruth, you go look in the mirror. You're lovely. And he has heard what kind of girl you are.*

Boaz told her:

"It has been fully reported to me, all that you have done for your mother-in-law since the death of your husband, and how you have left your father and your mother and the land of your birth, and have come to a people whom you did not know before."
(Ruth 2:11)

You see, when she had come to town, the little town of Bethlehem, the tongues were wagging, "Did you see Naomi and that little foreign girl with her? Ooooooo, is she good-looking!" And they said, "You just watch her, she'll start running after the men in town."

But she didn't. She accepted the fact that she was an outsider. But this man Boaz put his mantle of protection around her and said to her, "You glean in my field," and he made every move possible to win her. And he did win her.

I can answer her question, "Why have I found favor in your eyes?" But I cannot answer my question, "Why have *I* found grace in God's eyes?" Now don't tell me to go look in the mirror because I have, and the sight is not lovely. I have found grace in His eyes, not because of anything I am, but because of who He is. He has made a way for me by giving His Son to die on the cross. I got in because of grace. Marvelous, infinite, amazing grace.

Now I know that grace is defined by the theologian as unmerited favor. And I'll have to go along with that because who am I to go against theologians? But I'd like to add this: Grace is love in action. That's what grace is.

You can talk about loving, and that's all it can be, just talk. I remember the old story about the young fellow who wrote his girl a letter. He wanted to be poetic, and he was! He wrote, "I would swim the widest ocean for you. I'd climb the highest mountain for you. I'd crawl across the burning sands of the desert for you, and I would trudge through the snowstorm neck-deep for you." And then he put a little P.S. at the end of the letter: "If it doesn't rain next Wednesday night, I'll be over to see you." May I say to you, friend, there's a lot of talk about loving today, but not very much of it is being demonstrated.

Somebody loved Ruth. Somebody loved her so much that he was willing to risk everything for her. And he did. Boaz put his mantle of protection around her. He

put his arm of love around her and brought her as his
wife into the congregation of the Lord. What a story!
And God gave it on the human plane so that I could
understand, so that with my simple mind I could grasp
something of His love for me and for you.

When He came down to earth we were sinners. The
Law condemned us; the Law shut us out. No man can
take the Law or the Sermon on the Mount and look at
them honestly, then look at his own heart and say, "I
can stand before God, I've measured up to it all." God
says that you lie if you say that you can keep His Law.
If you say that you are without sin, you lie. The Law
shut me out, the Law condemned me. But God so loved
us that He gave His only begotten Son. God did not so
love the world that He saved the world. God so loved the
world that He gave His only begotten Son, that the
world of sinners might come to Him. My friend, you can
come now.

But you have to make up your own mind. It's up to
you. He has demonstrated His love to you. And if you
come and hold out the weak hand of faith—and nothing
else—He reaches down His mighty arm of salvation in
grace, and He lifts you up.

Free from the law, O happy condition.
Jesus hath bled and there is remission.
Cursed by the Law and bruised by the Fall,
Christ hath redeemed us once for all.

—P. P. Bliss

And John Greenleaf Whittier wrote:

The hour draws near,
  However delayed and late,
When, at the Eternal Gate,
  We leave the words and works we call our own,
And lift void hands alone
  For love to fill.

Our nakedness of soul
  Brings to that gate no toll,
Giftless we come to Him who all things gives,
  And live because He lives.

You see, God by love can't just reach down and arbitrarily and bigheartedly save. That is something the judges in this country need to learn—that the laws have to be enforced. God is not lawless. God cannot, in a softhearted way, say to the sinner, "It just breaks My heart—I can't punish you. You must come on into heaven." God never saves that way. God must punish sin.

"The soul who sins shall die . . ." (Ezekiel 18:20). God loves the sinner, and God had to provide a way for the Law to be satisfied. So His Son came and paid the penalty. Oh, to see that, my friend! He paid the penalty for your sins so that you could come into His presence, not as a pardoned criminal, but as one who is in Christ, with as much right in heaven as He has. I don't mean to be irreverent—for you do have His right. He did that because He loved you, but He had to provide a salvation for you.

And so it was with Ruth. She got into the genealogy of Christ because of grace, God's amazing grace.

BATHSHEBA—SECURITY

There is one more: Bathsheba.

And Jesse begot David the king. David the king begot Solomon by her who had been the wife of Uriah.
(Matthew 1:6)

Actually, Bathsheba's name is not given. I think that the Spirit of God, in wonderful reticence, omitted her name because the sin is not hers. It is David's sin. Yet he happens to be the man of whom God says, "He is a man after My own heart." How can that be, since God is a holy God? This account concerning Bathsheba reveals that we can have the assurance of salvation.

David never lost his salvation. He said in great confession, "Restore to me the joy of Your salvation" (Psalm 51:12a). He had lost his joy, but not his salvation.

Now look at it for just a moment. This man committed an awful sin (the record is in 2 Samuel, chapter 11). Can he get by with it? The king of Babylon could have gotten by with it, and did; the pharaoh of Egypt got by with it; the Caesars of Rome got by with it; and Hollywood and TV stars are getting by with it. But David cannot get by with it because he is God's man. That is the difference, I would say, between the sin of a believer and the sin of an unbeliever. If you are a child of God and commit sin, you will not get by with it. "Well," somebody says, "what about the sin of the unbeliever?" The devil whips his own children. God takes care of His, and He disciplines only His own.

After David had sinned, he sat back on his throne and

looked around, thinking, *I wonder if anybody knows*? In his confession he tells us:

> **When I kept silent, my bones grew old through my groaning all the day long. For day and night Your hand was heavy upon me; my vitality was turned into the drought of summer.**
> (Psalm 32:3, 4)

He says: "My bones ached!"

Oh, I tell you, a child of God when he sins, simply does not get by with it. The prodigal son, when he came to himself, said, "I want to get back to the father's house. I don't like the pigpen." If you like the pigpen, you are not God's child. You know, there is only one class that likes pigpens, and that's pigs. And it isn't the police who are pigs. It is the sinner without Christ. He loves the pigpen.

Now the child of God may get into the pigpen. David got in there, but he didn't stay there. Oh, he's disturbed! And he looks around, wondering if anybody knows. A lot of Christians are like that.

I have a letter from a man who told me of the burden that he'd been carrying. If you're God's child you've got to *talk* with somebody about your sin. And David is sitting there on his throne, and he looks over the crowd and says to himself: *I don't think they know, nobody's acting like they do.*

Then there's a lull in business, and Nathan the prophet steps up with a little story to tell the king. It went something like this:

"There happens to be two men in your kingdom that I'd like to tell you about. One has flocks and flocks of sheep and herds and herds of cattle. Living next door to him is a poor man who had only one little ewe lamb. A visitor came to this rich man and, in order to prepare a meal for his guest, the rich man killed that little ewe lamb. He had all these other sheep of his own, but he killed his poor neighbor's little pet lamb."

David—he was redheaded—rose up from his throne in anger. My, he's hot! It's interesting how easy it is for us to see the sin in other people's lives. The reason there's so much gossip in the church is that we can always see sin in the other fellow, can't we? And David rose up and said, "The man who has done this thing shall surely die! And he shall restore this lamb fourfold."

Nathan, in my opinion, is the bravest man in the Bible. He says, "You are the man!"

Do you know what David could have done? He could have been pious. "Me? Why, I would never do a thing like that. Take this man Nathan out and execute him!" And that would have ended it. But not for David. He is God's man. He has been suffering under the burden of unconfessed sin. His bones have been burning within him! He acknowledges his sin, and he goes and makes his confession: "I have sinned against the Lord." Then God says, "David, because you did this thing, you are causing the unbeliever, the heathen, to blaspheme Me."

And after more than 3,000 years, they still blaspheme God because of David's sin. Passing through Pershing Square in downtown Los Angeles one day, I heard an old blasphemer scoffing, "Imagine God taking that fellow David!" And, with a smirk, he added, "And they say He's a holy God."

One night that same old blasphemer sat in my congregation, and after the service he came to me with the same old tripe, sneering, "Why would God take a man like David?"

I said, "You'd better thank God that He would take a man like David, because if He will take David, He might take you and He might take me."

I thank God He did not give David up. David longed to come back to God and be in fellowship with Him. Reading his psalms convinces me that no one loved God more than David did. And God didn't throw him over. God received him. But God took him to the woodshed, and He never removed the lash from his back. Tragedy came. That first little one born of Bathsheba died. Later, one of his daughters was ruined; a son was guilty. Another son—the one he loved above all else, whom he had spoiled, the one David wanted to succeed him on the throne—this boy Absalom raised an insurrection against him.

David told Joab and the other captains of his army, "Spare my boy Absalom." And then he sat and waited. Finally he saw a runner coming with news of the battle. And the runner reported that the battle had been won!

But David's not interested in that. "What about my boy Absalom?"

The runner said, "I don't know."

Then came another runner; this one had news. When he got to where David was sitting, the king said to the runner, "What about my boy Absalom?"

The runner told him that Absalom was dead.

David took his great mantle and threw it over his face and, walking up the steps to the top of the wall, he wept.

And as he went, he said thus: "O my son Absalom—my son, my son Absalom—if only I had died in your place! O Absalom my son, my son!"
(2 Samuel 18:33*b*)

By this time I feel like saying to God, "Lord, You've whipped him enough." But David never said that. Neither did the Lord take the lash off his back.

Finally, as an old man sitting on the throne, David looked back over his life and said, "The LORD is my shepherd; I shall not want." I thank God He didn't throw David overboard. You can call it the perseverance of the saints; you can call it the security of the believer; but I say it is the assurance of salvation. I thank God that when the Lord Jesus saves us He doesn't save us for only a few days; He saves us for time and for eternity. And because we are His children, He won't let us live in sin. You won't find David committing that sin again and again. Do you know why? He belongs to God. He confessed his sin to God, and God brought him back into sweet fellowship with Himself. David did not lose his salvation.

Here in the genealogy of Christ is woven this wonderful story of salvation. The first step is to come as a sinner; the second step is to hold up the weak hand of faith; the third, God reaches down in grace and delivers us; the fourth, He saves us for time and eternity.

— 6 —

HOSEA

The Greatest Sin in All the World

Now we come to a very interesting story. The story behind the prophecy of the Old Testament Book of Hosea is the tragedy of a broken home. And to make it worse, it's the home of one of God's prophets. The personal experience of the prophet Hosea is the background of his message. It concerns the intimate affairs of his home. And the home is always given top priority in God's Word.

The home is the rock foundation of society, the most important unit in the social structure. It is to society and the state, to the church and to the nation what the atom is to the physical universe. The atom has been called the building block of the universe, and the home is exactly that.

You see homes stretching out in these new subdivisions like beads on a chain as you go up one street and down another. The home is the chain of a nation that runs up and down the streets of every city and every town and the highways and byways of the countryside. No chain is stronger than the links which compose it. Similarly, no nation is stronger than the homes which constitute its total population. And the home life of Hosea provides the background for his message to the nation of Israel.

The home is where we live, move, and have our being. It is in the home that we are truly ourselves. All of us dress up physically and psychologically when we go out, but within the walls of the place called home we remove our masks and show what we really are.

Because of the strategic position of the home, God has thrown about it certain safeguards to protect it. God has surrounded the home with a wall of instruction due to its importance. He has moved into the home to direct its intimate relationships. Actually, marriage is the very backbone of the home and has received more attention from God than any other institution.

Society never made marriage—it found it. God is the One who made marriage. It was His gift to mankind, and marriage rests upon His direct Word:

"Therefore what God has joined together, let not man separate."
(Mark 10:9)

God performed the first marriage ceremony. He gave away the first bride. He blessed the first couple. Marriage is more than a legal arrangement, even more than the union of mutual love. It is an act of God. It rests upon His fiat command. Too many young people think that all they need in order to get married is a license and a preacher. But, my friend, they need God. If He doesn't bless the union, it is not what God planned marriage to be. Oh, the love that God can bring to a marriage, the love of the man for the woman and the love of the woman for the man!

God has given a drive to the human race to reproduce within the framework of marriage and nowhere else: "And the two shall become one flesh" (Mark 10:8); "Be fruitful and multiply" (Genesis 1:28). Marriage is a sacred relationship and it is a holy union. The New Testament sums up the mind of God in this matter: "Marriage is honorable among all" (Hebrews 13:4*a*). Therefore, marriage cannot be broken by a legal act, a fit of temper, or self-will. There are only two acts which break marriage—that is, real marriage.

The first factor which breaks marriage is the death of either the husband or the wife.

> **For the woman who has a husband is bound by the law to her husband as long as he lives. But if the husband dies, she is released from the law of her husband.**
> (Romans 7:2)

This is accepted by all Christians as a legitimate breaking of the marriage relationship. But some zealous Christians use Romans 7:2 as the basis for the extreme viewpoint that a divorced person who has a living mate can never remarry. They forget that under the Law the married person who was guilty of fornication or adultery was stoned to death and was somewhere under a pile of rocks. So the innocent party under the Law did not have a living partner. Southern California would be covered with rock piles were the Mosaic Law enforced today!

The second act that breaks a marriage is unfaithfulness on the part of either the husband or the wife. This rips the relationship apart and drives a wedge into that which God has made one. Under the Mosaic system, a man or woman who was guilty of adultery was dealt with summarily. Such perfidy merited death, and it was meted out without mercy. Listen to the Law:

The man who commits adultery with another man's wife, he who commits adultery with his neighbor's wife, the adulterer and the adulteress, shall surely be put to death. (Leviticus 20:10)

Under the Mosaic Law when one was unfaithful, that spouse was eliminated, and as a result the other one would be free.

But if the thing is true, and evidences of virginity are not found for the young woman, then they shall bring out the young woman to the door of her father's house, and the men of her city shall stone her to death with stones, because she has done a disgraceful thing in Israel, to play the har-

lot in her father's house. So you shall put away the evil from among you.
(Deuteronomy 22:20, 21)

Another item concerning the Law which needs amplification is the reference in Deuteronomy which seems to preclude the man from any charge of guilt. The facts are that the analogy is to Christ and the church. Christ is never under suspicion—the church is. Also, it is true that the Law uses the masculine gender when it means either man or woman. The word is used as a generic term. That is, *mankind* means both men and women. Even today a legal document reads, "The party of the first part . . . if *he*" when the party of the first part may be *she*.

In spite of this explanation, there is a sense in which the Bible teaches a double standard. This does not mean there is a high standard for women and a low standard for men, but it does mean that they are different. This is an established custom which is under attack in our society. Yet every department store has a women's department and a men's department. Every hospital has a women's ward and a men's ward. This line of demarcation is recognized on every level of the social world. I believe that this is a valid distinction. For this same reason, I take my watch to one repairman and my car to another. The watch is a more delicate mechanism and needs the attention of a different mechanic with a different technique.

Woman is made finer than man. Therefore, it is more tragic when she goes wrong than when a man does. It is not that sin in one is worse than in another, but the

results are far more detrimental. In my limited ministry, I have seen children overcome the handicap of a
ne'er-do-well father, even a drunkard, but I have never
seen children turn out right with that kind of mother.
The poor performance of a father is a serious handicap
for a child, but a good mother can more than compensate. Mother is the center of the home. A godly mother
said some time ago, when she refused to accept an office
in a church organization, "I am a missionary to the
nursery, and there are three pairs of eyes watching me.
I want to direct them to God." It is more tragic when a
woman goes wrong than when a man goes wrong.

Alan Beck's definition of a little girl will, I believe,
give a fitting and intrinsic estimation of what I mean:

> Little girls are the nicest things that happen to
> people. They are born with a little bit of angel-shine
> about them, and, though it wears thin sometimes,
> there is always enough left to lasso your heart—
> even when they are sitting in the mud, or crying
> temperamental tears, or parading up the street in
> mother's best clothes.

> A little girl can be sweeter (and badder) oftener
> than anyone else in the world. She can jitter
> around, and stomp, and make funny noises and
> frazzle your nerves, yet just when you open your
> mouth, she stands there demure with that special
> look in her eyes. A girl is Innocence playing in the
> mud, Beauty standing on its head and Motherhood
> dragging a doll by the foot.

> God borrows from many creatures to make a little
> girl. He uses the song of a bird, the squeal of a pig,

the stubbornness of a mule, the antics of a monkey, the spryness of a grasshopper, the curiosity of a cat, the slyness of a fox, the softness of a kitten. And to top it off, He adds the mysterious mind of a woman.

A little girl likes new shoes, party dresses, small animals, dolls, make-believe, ice cream, make-up, going visiting, tea parties, and one boy. She doesn't care so much for visitors, boys in general, large dogs, hand-me-downs, straight chairs, vegetables, snowsuits, or staying in the front yard. She is loudest when you are thinking, prettiest when she has provoked you, busiest at bedtime, quietest when you want to show her off, and most flirtatious when she absolutely must not get the best of you again.

She can muss up your home, your hair, and your dignity—spend your money, your time, and your temper—then just when your patience is ready to crack, her sunshine peeks through and you've lost again.

Yes, she is a nerve-racking nuisance, just a noisy bundle of mischief. But when your dreams tumble down and the world is a mess; when it seems you are pretty much of a fool after all, she can make you a king when she climbs on your knee and whispers, "I love you best of all!"

May I say to you, friends, what a tragedy it is when that precious little girl becomes a woman who goes wrong. It is the worst thing that can happen in a home.

The prophecy of Hosea must be contrasted with God's ideal of marriage and of womanhood. God's revelation of marriage and His controls for it must be written in letters of light over the sordid story of Hosea's experience. Light on dark is the most effective method of contrast. Some years ago, many of our freeway markers and street signs were changed and enlarged. Instead of black letters on a white background, the new signs used white letters on a dark background. This is God's method also. He writes His revelation and salvation on the black background of man's sin. God's high standard must be written over Hosea's home; only then will we catch the message.

HOSEA'S HOME

Now we are prepared to examine the story behind the headlines in Hosea. In the hill country of Ephraim, in one of the many little towns not found on the maps of the world, lived two young people. One was a boy by the name of Hosea, the other was a girl by the name of Gomer. I would guess that they fell in love, the same story which has been repeated millions of times, but never grows old. Then the girl went bad for some unexplained reason. To suggest any explanation is to speculate. She even resorted to the oldest profession known to mankind. Hosea was brokenhearted, and shame filled his soul. He must have thought about his recourse to the Mosaic Law. He could have brought her before the elders of the town and demanded the Law be enforced. In that case she would have been stoned, for she had betrayed him. He would have been justified.

Does this remind you of another story which occurred in these same hills seven hundred years later? Another young man by the name of Joseph was engaged to a young lady named Mary. He thought of putting her

away privately instead of publicly stoning her. But
Mary was innocent of any wrongdoing. Gomer was not.
There was no question of Gomer's guilt as far as the
record is concerned.

The Book of Hosea opens at this juncture of the story.
It opens with the most startling and shocking statement
in the entire Bible:

**When the LORD began to speak by Hosea,
the LORD said to Hosea:**

**"Go, take yourself a wife of harlotry
And children of harlotry,
For the land has committed great harlotry
By departing from the LORD."**
(Hosea 1:2)

Some have not been willing to concede this as the
actual experience of the prophet and have dismissed
this strong language by calling it all an allegory. Such
trifling with the Word of God waters it down to a
harmless solution which is more sickening than stimu-
lating. Let's face it—God commanded Hosea to break
the Mosaic Law! The Law said to stone her, but God
said, "Go, marry her." The thing God commanded Hosea
to do must have caused him to revolt in every fiber of
his being. Where would God find a godly man today who
would go that far with Him?

Hosea did not demur—he obeyed explicitly. He took
Gomer in holy wedlock, and he gave her his name. She
came into his home as his wife. In the New Testament
we read:

> **Or do you not know that he who is joined to**
> **a harlot is one body with her? For "the two,"**
> **He says, "shall become one flesh."**
> (1 Corinthians 6:16)

You may be sure that the tempo of gossip was stepped up in their hometown. Someone has said that God made the country, and man made the city, but the devil made the little town. The gossip of folk in a little town is cruel and brutal, although they don't mean it to be. The mistake of an individual is known by all and forgotten by none. Hosea's home became a desert island in a sea of criticism, such as, "Can you imagine Hosea as God's man—and look who he has married!" What a tragic and awful thing took place there. It was segregation with a vengeance, for that man and his wife were shut off from society in that little town. A case of leprosy in the home would not have broken off contact with the outside world more effectively. Poor Hosea!

Into that home children were born. There were three, two boys and one girl. God named each of them, and the meaning of their names tells the awful story. And there is also the larger meaning and message for the nation Israel.

Jezreel was the oldest. His name means, "God will scatter." The reference is directly to a brutality in the life of Jehu for which there was no repentance (see 2 Kings 10). God is saying through this child Jezreel, "God will scatter Israel." But there will be mercy in His judgment, for there always is.

The second child was Lo-Ruhamah, which means "unpitied," implying that she never knew a father's pity.

It was not that she was an orphan, but there was a
question about who her father was. What a scandal in
the home of Hosea. But I want to say to you, it was a
message for the nation! That generation of Israel would
not know the pity of God, but God would remember to
be gracious to a later generation that He could call His
own.

The last child was Lo-Ammi, which means "not my
people." There is something very insinuating here
which I feel should be mentioned. If you put this in the
singular, it would mean "not my child." Hosea here is
frankly revealing the scandal of his home. Oh, God was
speaking to the nation, that nation which had aposta-
tized and departed from Him. He was saying to them,
as when the Pharisees came to the Lord Jesus and said,
"We are Abraham's descendants," our Lord replied,
"You are of your father the devil"—you are illegitimate
(see John 8:39–44).

Oh, how many church members are saying, "We are
the children of God," but they are illegitimate! They are
not His children at all. People say today that there is
the "universal fatherhood of God and the universal
brotherhood of man." That is the biggest lie and the
most damnable heresy that has ever been turned loose
in this world. Our Lord said to the religious leaders,
"You are of your father the devil." God says, "But as
many as received Him [the Lord Jesus Christ], to them
He gave the right to become children of God"—even to
those who don't do any more or less than simply "believe
in His name" (John 1:12). It is when you believe and
receive the Lord Jesus Christ as your Savior that you
become a child of God. And until you have come to Him

as a sinner and have accepted Him as your Savior who paid the penalty for your sins, you are an illegitimate child. You are Lo-Ammi, "not My child." How tragic it is to be deceived!

In the home of Hosea these three children tell its sad story, and in the larger sphere, they depict the declension of the northern kingdom of Israel which is called Ephraim in the Book of Hosea.

This does not end the record. Gomer ran away from home. She returned to her former profession. She became a common prostitute. You would think that now God would say, "Hosea, you have given her a chance, and obviously she is not going to be a faithful wife to you. You loved her and she betrayed you. Now I'll permit you to give her up." But God didn't say that.

> **Then the LORD said to me, "Go again, love a woman who is loved by a lover and is committing adultery, just like the love of the LORD for the children of Israel, who look to other gods and love the raisin cakes of the pagans."**
> (Hosea 3:1)

As women of this sort did in those days, she had sold herself into slavery:

> **So I bought her for myself for fifteen shekels of silver, and one and one-half homers of barley.**
> (Hosea 3:2)

It would indeed be gratifying to be able to say that she became a good wife and mother and they lived happily ever after. Certainly, by inference, that is the conclusion that I drew, since the analogy is to Israel:

For the children of Israel shall abide many days without king or prince, without sacrifice or sacred pillar, without ephod or teraphim. Afterward the children of Israel shall return and seek the LORD their God and David their king. They shall fear the LORD and His goodness in the latter days.
(Hosea 3:4, 5)

Finally God will triumph with the nation. The victory of love is the theme of the Book of Hosea.

PREPARED TO PREACH

This concludes the personal history of Hosea. It is a sordid and sorry account of the domestic affairs of God's prophet. For the sake of poetic justice, perhaps we should say that Hosea saved his home. This, however, is not the purpose of recording his experience. God was disciplining this man to speak on His behalf to a nation that was guilty of spiritual adultery. Out of a home scarred by shame, this man stepped before the nation with a message of fire! He stood before his people with a heartbreak that was intolerable, with scalding tears coursing down his cheeks, an ache of soul and a shame of spirit, to *denounce* a people who were guilty of religious harlotry! He walked out of a home broken by sin and scandal; a home saddened, soiled, and sullied by the ugliness of sin. And I like what Dean Plumptre wrote years ago—as though Hosea were speaking:

> *Now I sit*
> *All lonely, homeless, weary of my life,*
> *Thick darkness round me, and the stars all*
> *   dumb*
> *That erst had sung their wondrous tale of joy.*
> *And thou hadst done it all, O faithless one!*
> *O Gomer! Whom I loved as never wife*
> *Was loved in Israel, all the wrong is thine!*
> *Thy hand hath spoiled all my tender vines,*
> *Thy foot hath trampled all my pleasant fruits,*
> *Thy sin hath laid my honor in the dust.*

Hosea was God's man who denounced the nation and declared a verdict of guilty for the crime of crimes. He said simply but specifically that sin is as black as can be and that God will punish sin wherever He finds it.

Yet God loves the sinner. When a nation acknowledges God and turns to Him, is blessed of Him, and experiences His love, then subsequently turns from Him to idols, the sin of that nation is labeled spiritual harlotry.

God took Israel out of Egypt. He led its people through the wilderness, and His own explanation was:

"You have seen what I did to the Egyptians, and how I bore you on eagles' wings and brought you to Myself."
(Exodus 19:4)

Yet this people made themselves a golden calf to worship and turned away from the God who loved them. At that time, God brought them back to Himself.

Many years later after the kingdom of Israel divided, the northern kingdom—to whom Hosea was speaking—made two golden calves and again turned to calf worship. And again God attempted to woo them back to Himself, but they would not. The charge made repeatedly against them was that they went whoring after other gods. Candidly stated, the charge was that Israel was playing the harlot. This is sin at its worst. However, I don't want to be misunderstood. I am not suggesting the sensational idea that the breaking of the seventh commandment is the chief sin—that's not it.

WHAT IS THE GREATEST SIN?

I am now ready to ask the question and attempt to answer it: "What is the greatest sin in all the world?" Well, in the past, two have been suggested which are worth consideration as the greatest. One is *unbelief.* Many say that unbelief is absolutely the greatest sin. It is true that there is no remedy for unbelief. God has a remedy for all sin, but unbelief means to reject the remedy. Nevertheless, multitudes are in unbelief because they have never heard that the Son of God has paid the penalty for their sins. When they hear, they will believe. Others have honest doubts. The honest doubter is a rare specimen, but I myself came that route, and I believe that all who have an honest doubt will eventually come to faith in Christ. God is prepared to deal with them. It is the dishonest doubter who gives one excuse when he has a different one in his heart—

God will not deal with him. Unbelief is not the greatest sin.

Others hold that *sin against light* is the chief sin. This is coming close, but it misses the mark. Surely the people of Israel had light, and light does add to the exceeding sinfulness of sin—God dealt with them on that basis. In the economy of God, it is difficult to say that there is one sin that is worse than any other when God says:

For whoever shall keep the whole law, and yet stumble in one point, he is guilty of all. (James 2:10)

Our Lord Himself said that when the Holy Spirit comes, "He will convict the world of sin . . . because they do not believe in Me" (John 16:8, 9). And if a man or nation has had the light of God and then rejects it, that makes their sin worse. The sin of America is worse than the sin of China. I would much rather be an idolater in the darkness of some tropical jungle, bowing down in fear before an idol, than to be a cynic who sits within the sound of the gospel in any Bible-believing church from Sunday to Sunday without responding to God's invitation and without receiving the light of heaven. Yes, sin against light is heinous. There is, however, a sin that is even greater.

The greatest sin in all the world is sin against love. This is sin at its worst. And this is the revelation of Hosea. Gomer was not only guilty of breaking the marriage vow, but she sinned against the one who loved her. That is unspeakable. That is worse than the animism and animalism of the heathen world. It is deeper and darker than the immorality of the underworld and the demonism of the overworld. Hosea knew what sin was, and he knew what love was. He knew what the greatest sin in all the world was from personal experience. Hosea walked out before the nation of Israel to give them God's message and could say in substance, "I know how God feels. God's heart is broken. I know because my heart is broken. I have loved this woman, but she betrayed me. And God loves you, and you have betrayed Him." That is sin at its worst. You can't get any lower than that, my beloved. Sin against love aggravates sin. Israel had known the love of God. She had experienced His deliverance, His redemption, His protection, His forgiveness, His revelation, and His unconditional love. Israel turned to dumb idols and gave herself to them. This was sin against love, and nothing was worse. But God would not give her up; love will triumph!

God says that He will get the victory. The story is told in three verses in the Book of Hosea.

Here is the charge:

**"Ephraim is joined to idols,
Let him alone."**
(Hosea 4:17)

God says to Hosea, "Let them alone. They've gone after idols," but Hosea could say, "O Lord, You sent me out to get Gomer and bring her back; what are You going to do with these people?" God says, "I'll go get them."

Here is the pulsating passion of our God:

> **"How can I give you up, Ephraim?**
> **How can I hand you over, Israel?**
> **How can I make you like Admah?**
> **How can I set you like Zeboiim?**
> **My heart churns within Me;**
> **My sympathy is stirred."**
> (Hosea 11:8)

In essence God says, "My thought was to judge you and to scatter you, even now," but He says, "I love you too much, and I am sending Hosea to you again. He knows how I feel because I've let him feel the same way. He will tell you that I love you in spite of all your failure, in spite of committing the worst sin of all, sinning against My love."

Here is victory:

> **"Ephraim shall say,**
> **'What have I to do anymore with idols?'**
> **I have heard and observed him.**
> **I am like a green cypress tree;**
> **Your fruit is found in Me."**
> (Hosea 14:8)

In other words, "I'll no longer play the harlot, I'm through with idols. I'll be faithful to God." There will come a day when Israel will turn from idols back to God. And may I say, this has a message for our day.

When a young couple has made shipwreck of their marriage and then comes to me, my first inquiry concerns their personal relationship. Recently a young couple came to me with their problem. I asked them if they still loved each other. Tears filled their eyes, and they confessed eagerly that they did. It is unnecessary to say that they are working out their problem. When love is gone, it looks hopeless, but with love there is hope.

Does this shocking description of spiritual adultery fit the church? The church is described as the bride of Christ: "I have betrothed you . . . that I may present you as a chaste virgin to Christ" (2 Corinthians 11:2). To the Ephesian church our Lord said, "I have this against you, that you have left your first love" (Revelation 2:4*b*). It is also interesting to note that the Hebrew name *Hosea* means "salvation" and is another form of the name *Joshua*. The Hebrew name *Joshua* in the Old Testament is in the Greek form *Jesus* in the New Testament:

"You shall call His name JESUS, for He will save His people from their sins."
(Matthew 1:21)

Therefore, Jesus is the modern Hosea and the church is the bride of Christ. But is she faithful to Him today? Playing and toying with the world even now, she is being molded into its lifestyle and has become lukewarm in her relationship with Christ. Our Lord Jesus said to the church of Laodicea, which I'm convinced represents the church of the present hour:

"I know your works, that you are neither cold nor hot. I could wish you were cold or hot. So then, because you are lukewarm, and neither cold nor hot, I will vomit you out of My mouth."
(Revelation 3:15, 16)

In other words, He says, "You are playing the harlot." Does that disturb you? The harlotry of worldliness is the besetting sin of the church today.

Now let us bring this down to the individual. What is your personal relationship with Jesus Christ? Has a cloud come between you and Him? Has some sin eclipsed His presence? Are you indifferent? Are you trying to compensate by criticizing or turning to some feverish service? Before the Lord Jesus put Simon Peter in harness, He asked the heart-searching question, "Do you love Me?" This is just as poignant and pertinent now as it was that early dawn by the Sea of Galilee, for He calls you by name today. He is not interested in your service or the outward testimony you are giving. He is asking you in your heart of hearts, "Do you love Me?"

— 7 —

MARY

The First Person to Doubt the Virgin Birth

Someone in the dim and distant past observed that the story of every great man began with his mother. Long before modern science discovered the importance of heredity, we find that the story of Jesus begins with His mother.

The choice of Mary to mother the Messiah was not by chance or by accident. There is about this girl a personal goodness and nobility of character that far exceeds the average. There is a simplicity and sweetness that is refreshing and attractive. I wish that we could forget how she looks on a Christmas card and how she looks in a plaster cast model, and think of her as a very refreshing young girl who lived in the little town of Nazareth. May I say to you, she was a wholesome, sweet, wonderful person. She's no queen of heaven or the object of veneration or worship, but there is a danger for Protestants, in rebounding from that sort of idolatry, to brush her aside and treat her story as being incidental.

It is my desire today to handle the Christmas story with reverence and tenderness, which is the only way it should be treated. Dr. G. Campbell Morgan, in speaking of this story, says it is "matchless, mysterious, magnificent and majestic." And I'd like to add that it is all that and more.

The Gospel of Luke begins the record with the visit of the angel Gabriel sent by God to Zacharias, a priest in the temple at Jerusalem. And Gabriel announced to him that he would father the child who would become John the Baptist. Zacharias found it difficult to believe this message from God.

Now we come to the second visit of Gabriel. This time he will not only bypass Rome, the political power center of the world, but he's going to bypass the temple and the priesthood and come to the despised province of Galilee, to the little town of Nazareth. He is coming to a humble peasant girl with a startling announcement—an announcement that every Hebrew woman would have given anything to hear. It was the fulfillment of a promise God had made and that many Old Testament prophets had said would come to pass.

I'm turning to an unusual prophecy that's found in Isaiah 9:1, 2 which pinpoints Galilee as the area where the message would be given. It identifies it like this: "By the way of the sea, beyond the Jordan, in Galilee of the Gentiles." At this time, Nazareth is going to be made glorious up yonder by the way of the sea, where "the people who walked in darkness [would see] a great light." This place is to become one of the three focal points around the birth of the Lord Jesus. First it was Bethlehem and now it's Nazareth. Later it will be Egypt.

Now notice how the story opens:

Now in the sixth month the angel Gabriel was sent by God to a city of Galilee named Nazareth, to a virgin betrothed to a man whose name was Joseph, of the house of David. The virgin's name was Mary.
(Luke 1:26, 27)

We will see that when God moves in Nazareth, He touches the simple life, and He makes it sublime. He touches the natural with the supernatural. He comes to the ordinary and makes it extraordinary. He takes the commonplace and makes it an out-of-this-world place, if you please.

Most people in that day thought history was being made in Rome, the great power center. There were others who thought that history was being made in Athens, the cultural center. Still others thought that Jerusalem, the religious center, was the place where history was being made. My beloved, Nazareth, an unknown center, was the place that was to become world famous. There are very few people who can tell you what happened in Rome or Athens or Jerusalem at this particular time, but the whole world has heard a little something about Nazareth. Sometimes we get a wrong perspective of things. May I say to you, and I say it kindly, what happened in the White House yesterday will be forgotten in fifty years, and nobody will even know what happened. But what happened in a stable in Bethlehem about 2,000 years ago will never be forgotten. God will see to that.

As we read in Isaiah 9, the prophet pinpointed this event yonder in the land beyond the River Jordan "by the way of the sea"—around that little Sea of Galilee— and Nazareth is in that area.

Now here is the salutation of Gabriel to Mary:

And having come in, the angel said to her, "Rejoice, highly favored one, the Lord is with you; blessed are you among women!" (Luke 1:28)

I'd have you note several things that are stated here. The first thing is that this word "highly favored" is an expression, but actually the Greek word is *grace*. It has given the impression that the angel was speaking of the wonderful office Mary was to fulfill, but it has no reference to the office at all. Rather, it is a description of her character. You will notice in most Bibles certain words are printed in italics that are not in the original text but were added to make a smooth translation. Sometimes it is clearer without them, and this is an example. Mary was endued with grace: "Hail, graced one! The Lord is with you." It has to do with the character of this young person, Mary. It's a thumbnail portrait, actually, of her. Here she was, living in Nazareth, a little-known place. It's called "Galilee of the Gentiles" because the main highway between what is known today as Lebanon and

Jerusalem came down through there within about half a mile of Nazareth. Folk of all nations passed over that road. Soldiers were billeted nearby. It was a place that was sunken in iniquity.

The wonderful thing is that God sends the angel to Nazareth. In the midst of the corruption of that town, this peasant maiden in the royal line of David has been kept from the impurity of that place and that time. She stands out like a jewel in the little town of Nazareth. That's one of the remarkable things about her, and you'll notice how Gabriel addressed her. Dr. Luke, a physician in the first century, was chosen by God to give us these details for good reason. Speaking of Mary and identifying her, he says she is "a virgin betrothed to a man whose name was Joseph." May I say this to you today, the word *virgin*—used twice in verse 27—does not have two meanings. It means only one thing. Those who do not want to accept the virgin birth of Jesus like to argue about the meaning of words. You can't argue about the meaning of words with Dr. Luke. He uses the Greek word *parthenos*, and so does Matthew. The word *parthenos* means "virgin." It was the name given to that lovely temple yonder in Athens called the Parthenon, built to the virgin goddess Athena. Had you asked any Greek walking down the street about Athena, he would have been very quick to tell you that she was a virgin, and there would have been no question about what was meant. My friend, the virgin birth of Jesus was not questioned by the church until centuries later when some dirty-minded theologian came along. But there's no misunderstanding what Dr. Luke is talking about—

and he's a doctor and will lay it on the line for us today. We cannot misunderstand what he has to say.

When Gabriel appears to Mary and makes this statement to her, notice her response:

But when she saw him, she was troubled at his saying, and considered what manner of greeting this was.
(Luke 1:29)

Now the reaction here of Mary is the same as Zacharias' back in verse 12 when Zacharias saw Gabriel. "He was troubled, and fear fell upon him." The word *troubled* as we understand the word doesn't quite convey the meaning. There is a word that's being used a great deal today, the word *disturbed*. We hear about many disturbed people in our contemporary society, and I think *disturbed* is the word that better describes Mary's feelings. She was not disturbed by the presence of the angel. Remember, this girl was brought up, as we shall see, on the Old Testament and she believed in the integrity of the Word of God. She believed in angels, she believed in the resurrection—she believed in these supernatural things. It was not the presence of the angel that disturbed her, but the greeting of the angel and the way he addressed her did disturb her. Notice, the angel said to her, "Do not be afraid, Mary, for you have found favor with God." And we're going to see in a moment that this is all-important.

This girl was disturbed because she was actually not aware of her beauty. She was not aware of the beauty of her character, nor was she aware of her sweet spirit—

and part of Mary's beauty was that she was unaware of it. That's the reason she was disturbed at Gabriel's greeting to her.

When the angel explained, "Do not be afraid, Mary, for you have found favor with God," it could be translated that she had found grace with God. To be technical, in this case the Greek preposition is *para*, meaning "by the side of." It has no reference here to character, but it does have reference to the fact that here is a woman who is having fellowship with God. In other words, the angel is saying, "Mary, you found favor with God because of who you are; and because of your having fellowship with Him, He has this message for you."

Now will you notice the message:

"And behold, you will conceive in your womb and bring forth a Son, and shall call His name JESUS. He will be great, and will be called the Son of the Highest; and the Lord God will give Him the throne of His father David. And He will reign over the house of Jacob forever, and of His kingdom there will be no end."
(Luke 1:31–33)

This is the message of the angel Gabriel to Mary. Will you notice it carefully: "and shall call His name JESUS." Because Mary knew the Old Testament, that took her back to Genesis, back to the Garden of Eden when Adam and Eve disobeyed God. God had said to the serpent who had been the instrument of Satan and was responsible for their fall into disobedience:

"And I will put enmity between you [Satan]
and the woman, and between your seed and
her Seed; He [Christ] **shall bruise your head,**
and you shall bruise His heel."
(Genesis 3:15)

Coming down through the centuries, this promise in
the Word of God begins to close in. First it was given to
the line of Abraham, and he was to be a blessing to all
peoples (see Genesis 12:2, 3). Then it was confined to
the tribe of Judah, "The scepter shall not depart from
Judah . . . until Shiloh comes . . ." (Genesis 49:10). Next
it was confined to the family of David, and finally
confined to a virgin who shall conceive. And now the
angel says to Mary, "You shall call His name JESUS,"
meaning "the Lord is salvation." He's the Seed of the
woman who was to come into the world to be the Savior
of the world. That's the reason He is given this name,
Jesus, the human name.

And then the second thing that Gabriel tells her is
that this Jesus is the Son of the Highest. And John in
his Gospel develops the record of Christ's incarnation
which we call the Christmas story. There he says, "The
Word became flesh." In other words, the angel Gabriel
says, "Though you are going to have a Son with the
human name of Jesus, He will be the Son of the Highest
[the Word become flesh], and He shall sit on the throne
of His father David!"

That was the heartbeat of the Old Testament. This
man David—you can criticize him, but he had a heart
and a passion for God. In Psalm 42:1 he says, "As the
deer pants for the water brooks, so pants my soul for

You, O God." How he loved God! Oh, the enthusiasm that he had for God and the things of God. He lived in a brutal, rough age; and when he finally took Jerusalem, he moved the Ark of the Covenant up there. One night it rained, and he was living in the new palace that Hiram had built for him. He could hear the rain pitter-patter outside and thought, "The ark of God is out there in a tent and here I am living in luxury." You don't find many folk with that kind of concern for God today. David called in the prophet Nathan the next morning and said, "Nathan, I'm going to build God a house," and even Nathan said, "Go ahead and do it." Here's a case when a prophet was wrong. God appeared to Nathan that night and said, "Look, Nathan, you're wrong. You go back and tell David he can't build Me a house because he has bloody hands. I can't use him for that reason, but I'll give him credit for it." My friend, you can never do anything for God but what He does something better for you. The Lord in substance said, "Does David want to build Me a house? Then I'm going to build David a house—and I mean a house." Think about what this meant! I'll lift out only three verses:

> **"When your days are fulfilled and you rest with your fathers, I will set up your seed after you, who will come from your body, and I will establish his kingdom. He shall build a house for My name, and I will establish the throne of his kingdom forever. . . . And your house and your kingdom shall be established forever before you. Your throne shall be established forever."**
> (2 Samuel 7:12, 13, 16)

Now centuries later, the angel Gabriel says to Mary, "And He [the child you shall bear] will reign over the house of Jacob forever, and of His kingdom there will be no end." The fulfillment of all that God had promised is now brought to a focal point yonder in Nazareth.

God's age-old promise of the coming Messiah is well known to Mary, and she is in fellowship with Him. So notice the reaction of this girl:

Then said Mary unto the angel, "How can this be, since I do not know a man?"
(Luke 1:34)

Without a moment's hesitation and with transparent simplicity, she artlessly and honestly and sincerely raises the first objection to the virgin birth. Do you want to know who first doubted the virgin birth? It was Mary herself. The angel Gabriel said, "You're going to have a Son." She said, "How can this be, since I do not know a man?" That's plain, unadorned, unabashed language. There's no false modesty here—and I consider puerile the translation of these sissy theologians who came along and translated it like this, "How can this be, seeing I'm an unmarried woman?" May I say to you, my friend, that's not what she said.

Now, this sophisticated age which has majored in sex will be able to understand this perplexing problem, because they all know about sex today. They talk about it on campuses, they talk about it on the street, it is thrown at them on television and in every newspaper and every magazine they see. Mary raised an obvious question: How can this be, since I do not know a man?

Will you listen to the angel Gabriel. He's going to answer, and remember that it was Dr. Luke who reported this:

And the angel answered and said to her, "The Holy Spirit will come upon you, and the power of the Highest will overshadow you; therefore, also, that Holy One who is to be born will be called the Son of God."
(Luke 1:35)

Now the angel Gabriel answers in terms, likewise, that cannot be misunderstood. Dr. Luke, who was a physician—Paul calls him "the beloved physician," and I think he was a Gentile—dealt in obstetrics. He gives the longest, most detailed account of the virgin birth.

Gabriel answers the biological question which Mary raised. That's the first part of the verse. We need to pay attention to it. "And the angel answered, and said unto her, 'The Holy Spirit will come upon you, and the power of the Highest will overshadow you.'" When Dr. Luke began writing his Gospel of Luke, he mentioned in the second verse that the reason he'd taken this project in hand was to record the information he had obtained from those who knew the facts—"Even as they delivered them unto us, who from the beginning were eyewitnesses" (see Luke 1:2). That word *eyewitnesses* is a medical term. In the Greek it's *autoptai,* "to see for yourself." Does *autoptai* sound like a word that you've heard before? *Autopsy.* Actually Dr. Luke says, "I made an autopsy of Jesus." As a physician of the first century, Dr. Luke uses more medical terms in his writings than Hippocrates, the founder of medicine.

Will you note this very carefully. In substance, Dr. Luke is saying this: *The birth of Jesus is supernatural.* You don't like that? Well, that's what he said. Can't someone explain it? No, we can't explain it. It is supernatural. "The angel answered and said to her, 'The Holy Spirit will come upon you, and the power of the Highest will overshadow you.'"

Now there's another question here that was not raised by Mary. It is a theological question—some call it a moral question. I'll be honest with you, it is the *big* question, and I doubt that it even entered the thinking of Mary at that time. The problem is what we call the doctrine of original sin, a total depravity of man, and that the father and the mother transmit to the child a sinful nature. Jesus did not have a sinful nature. Why didn't He? And how could He get a nature that is sinless by human birth? That's a problem.

Here in Southern California we have a constant itch for something new, and, as I write this, another explanation is making the rounds concerning the virgin birth of Jesus. I have received from two or three nurses and some laymen reams of paper explaining it to me. The only thing is, it doesn't explain it to me. Their theory is that when a baby is formed in a mother's womb it receives no blood from the mother and therefore Mary did not pass down to Jesus a sinful nature. Now I don't want to tear down any dollhouses, but if you can explain the birth of Jesus by any natural process, then it's not the explanation that Dr. Luke is giving. Let's understand that point. This is something that even the leading liberals ought to be able to understand today. I would say that the Harvard School of Religion ought to be able to get this. Dr. Luke makes it abundantly clear that the birth of Jesus was supernatural, that it was not natural at all.

In the first part of verse 35, Luke gives the biological explanation. In the last part he answers the theological or the moral problem. Listen to this: "Therefore, also, that Holy One who is to be born will be called the Son of God." I don't care how much blood He did or did not get—that's not the question. The Spirit of God saw to it that He is that "Holy One" and, my friend, that is supernatural. Don't miss the point. We're dealing with the supernatural here, and these little natural explanations that come along to bolster up the virgin birth are not worthwhile. God is holding this scientific, sophisticated, skeptical, and cynical age to only one point—the supernatural. Either you believe it or you don't believe it.

Do you know that man can't even explain the origin of life today? It's rather amusing that in the magazine section of our newspapers—they have to have something to fill them up—periodically an article comes out about scientists being right on the verge of discovering the origin of life. I read one the other day claiming they are right on the verge. But they have been on the verge ever since I have been reading, and I've been reading for a long time. I say to you that until man can answer the simple question of how a little tadpole began, then he's not even in a position to discuss the virgin birth of Jesus Christ—he doesn't *know* enough to discuss the virgin birth of the Lord Jesus Christ. God today is saying to the human family, "This is the naked Word of God. I present His birth as being supernatural. Take it or leave it." Do you believe it? You have nothing in the world to stand upon but the Word of God.

Will you consider verse 37 now, for this, to my judgment, is the key to the passage, and it is a verse that is generally passed over: "For with God nothing will be impossible." That's the explanation of the virgin birth: With God nothing will be impossible.

Dr. Luke, in the first century, recorded Christ's virgin birth. Moving down through about 1,900 years of history, you come to another medical man—a man from Johns Hopkins University—who even today is considered the greatest gynecologist who ever lived. While in the office of an obstetrician, an outstanding man here in Southern California, I noted on his bookshelves the name of Dr. Howard Kelly on a whole set of volumes. When the obstetrician came in, I said, "I noticed you have books by Dr. Howard Kelly." He said, "Yes, that's our bible. He's the authority on natural birth."

Well, Dr. Howard Kelly wrote also on the virgin birth of Jesus because he believed it. All the way from Dr. Luke to Dr. Howard Kelly, there is a host of medical men who have believed in His virgin birth. I do not know about you, but I want to say to you that I will take these men's word ahead of those theologians and educators who say that the virgin birth is a biological impossibility. They may be brilliant men, but they simply do not know anything about virgin birth, for with God nothing is impossible.

Now notice the next verse; it is the loveliest part of all:

Then Mary said, "Behold the maidservant
of the Lord! Let it be to me according to
your word." And the angel departed from
her.
(Luke 1:38)

When Mary said that, her life passed under a cloud,
and for thirty-three years the fact of the virgin birth
was questioned by the world around her. Oh, how she
wanted out from under that cloud. Yonder at the
wedding at Cana of Galilee she said to Jesus, "They
have no wine," and He knew what she meant. I believe
that she was saying, "Perform a miracle—this would
be an appropriate occasion." He answered, "Woman,
My hour has not yet come." His implication was,
"Wait, this is not the occasion. I'll clear your name,
but not here."

Three years went by and now He's hanging on a cross.
He looks down at His mother and says, "Woman, behold
your Son, My hour has come." And if you follow her, you
will read that she saw Him die, but when she went to
the tomb to anoint His body for burial, He was back from
the dead. She saw Him alive again, and she met with
the disciples yonder in the Upper Room. Honestly, I
don't think she ever fully understood until the Day of
Pentecost what all was involved. The resurrection
proves Jesus' virgin birth, you see. We tend to look at
the virgin birth at Christmas as an isolated fact. It is
connected with His resurrection, friend, because He is
who He claimed to be—truly the Son of God.

You remember when those shepherds came to the
manger to see Him and left rejoicing? Mary pondered

those things in her heart. She never knew. But on the Day of Pentecost, she knew.

Oh, the beauty and the loveliness of her life and the tenderness of her story! She obeyed God. "Behold the maidservant of the Lord!" The first word of Christmas is *faith,* the second word of Christmas is *obedience.* Obedience.

I'd like for you to see something more. The greatest document that we have on salvation is the Epistle to the Romans, and God put parentheses around Romans. Read it in chapter 1, verse 5:

> **Through Him we have received grace and apostleship for obedience to the faith among all nations for His name.**

That's at the first of the epistle. If you go to the end of Romans, you'll read:

> **Now to Him who is able to establish you according to my gospel and the preaching of Jesus Christ, according to the revelation of the mystery kept secret since the world began but now made manifest, and by the prophetic Scriptures made known to all nations, according to the commandment of the everlasting God, for obedience to the faith.**
> (Romans 16:25, 26)

At the beginning of Romans it's obedience to the faith; at the end of Romans it's obedience to the faith. That's what the Epistle of James is talking about also. It is not discussing salvation by works—it is discussing salva-

tion by faith. Note carefully James 2:18: ". . . Show me
your faith without your works, and I will show you my
faith by my works." Real living faith leads to obedience.
And if it doesn't, it is not real living faith.

Mary could have received the message brought to her
by the angel and said, "Now this is nice of you to call on
me, I consider it a great honor, but I don't think I'm
willing to take the assignment. It would cost me too
much." But Mary believed God. How do I know she
believed God? Because of her response: "Behold the
maidservant of the Lord!"

My friend, do you believe God today? Honestly, it's
not even a question of your believing the virgin birth.
You can believe it and still be lost. The question is, do
you have a faith in God that leads to obedience? There
are a lot of folk today who talk about faith and have a
lot of pious platitudes in their lives. But a living faith
leads to obedience to the Lord Jesus Christ, and if it
doesn't lead to obedience to Him, it's not a living faith.

There are a lot of Christians who are like the beautiful tree that stands in your home at Christmastime. It's
a lovely tree—don't misunderstand—but that's the pho-
niest thing there is. Do you think those lovely balls grow
on that tree? Of course they don't. It's a phoney. Do you
think that tree is alive? No. When they went into the
woods, they cut down that fine-looking tree because it was
shaped better than those about it. But out yonder on the
mountainside right now there is a little fir tree with no
beautiful decorations—its limbs are bent down by the
wind whipping through it, but it has life, it has virility.
But that decorated Christmas tree is dead as a doornail.

My friend, there are a lot of Christians like that.

They've got all the bangles, they've got all the sparkles, they've got all the cliches, but they do not have a faith that is living and leads to obedience. Oh, that is so important. Until it leads to obedience, you may be pretty, you may be attractive, but, as Calvin said, "Faith that saves is not alone, but faith alone saves." Let us pray.

Our gracious Father God, may this be a time of not decorating the outside of our lives, but may we lay bare our inmost soul for Thee as this simple girl yonder in Nazareth did. Oh, God, return us to these simplicities. Many of us today are sophisticated saints—we know all the answers, we know when to say amen and praise the Lord. But oh, God, how empty our lives are! How rebellious our hearts today, and even now there may be rebellion against a message that has called to obedience. Oh, God, today search our hearts, and if the Lord Jesus Christ is not born in our hearts, may He be born again in our own lives by the working of the Spirit of God, for we pray in Jesus' name, amen.

— 8 —

NICODEMUS

The Man Behind the Mask

There was a man of the Pharisees named Nicodemus, a ruler of the Jews.
(John 3:1)

I would like you to know this man Nicodemus, get acquainted with him. Note the three things said about him. The Spirit of God has a way of giving a biography by saying only three things. You and I don't do it that way. He has a way of putting things together so that the three things He says about this man are all we need to know.

The third chapter of John's Gospel records the most important message that any church in the entire world has to give. But the third chapter actually begins back in the second chapter, and we will start with verse 23.

> **Now when He was in Jerusalem at the Pass-
> over, during the feast, many believed in His
> name when they saw the signs which He
> did. But Jesus did not commit Himself to
> them, because He knew all men, and had no
> need that anyone should testify of man, for
> He knew what was in man.**
> (John 2:23–25)

That is a very remarkable passage and certainly a
fitting introduction to the man behind the mask.

Now the Lord Jesus had come up to Jerusalem for the
first time as He began His ministry. He had cleansed
the temple and He had healed multitudes. Many of the
people, we are told, believed in Him. To be very frank
with you, I would have recorded all these people as
converts if I'd been there. But we are told by John that
Jesus did not commit Himself to them. Literally, He did
not believe in them. They believed in Him, but He did
not believe in them because their faith rested on the fact
that He was a miracle worker rather than on the fact
that He was a Savior. And He didn't want that kind of
follower. So we're told that He did not commit Himself
to that crowd for the reason that He knew what was *in*
man, and He did not need anybody to testify of man.
You see, you needn't go to Jesus and say to Him, "Mr.
So-and-So is this or that kind of man"—He already
knows it. May I say to you that here we have something
that is quite remarkable.

Now, "There was a man of the Pharisees. . . ." This
man the Lord Jesus trusted, and that night He revealed
to him something that He had not revealed even to His

apostles, and He did not reveal it to them until two and a half years later. When they were in Caesarea Philippi six months before He went to Jerusalem, the Lord Jesus said to His apostles, "We are going to Jerusalem, and I'm going to die." And did they believe it? No. Simon Peter said, "Far be that from You, Lord. We're interested in a kingdom, not Your death." They didn't comprehend it at first. Five times on the way down to Jerusalem Jesus repeated it. And it finally got through to them that He was going to die upon a Roman cross for the sins of the world. The remarkable thing is that He revealed it at the very beginning to Nicodemus.

Many years ago, there was a man here in Southern California who wrote biographies of preachers, and one day I met him on the street in Pasadena. I asked whose biography he was writing, and he told me. So I asked, "How are you getting along?"

"I'm having a lot of trouble."

"What's the trouble?"

"Keeping the back page from rubbing against the front page—there's not much to say about that man."

"But the Holy Spirit can write all we need to know about a person in only three short sentences."

"Well, I'm not the Holy Spirit, and I have to write it differently."

Now notice the three things said about Nicodemus. He was a man of the Pharisees, that's number one. Second, his name was Nicodemus, and third, he was a ruler of the Jews.

I want to submit to you that this man functioned like that in life. When he came to the Lord Jesus he was wearing a mask. The Lord Jesus removed that mask because He deals with us just as we are, not behind a mask. Now let's examine this brief biography of Nicodemus. He was a man of the Pharisees, his name was Nicodemus, and he was a ruler of the Jews.

HE WAS A MAN OF THE PHARISEES

The Pharisees represented the best in Israel at that time. They were a religio-political party. As a religious party they were conservative. They believed in the Old Testament miracles. They believed in the integrity of Scripture. They believed in the resurrection. As a political party, they wanted to get rid of Rome. They wanted to throw off the yoke of Rome and establish the Davidic kingdom again here upon this earth. That was the way they moved, and this man Nicodemus was a man of the Pharisees. He moved out among the people, and when he went by they would say, "That's Nicodemus, he's a man of the Pharisees." And they thought they knew him, but actually underneath they did not actually know him.

HE WAS A RULER OF THE JEWS

He met with the Sanhedrin which meant he was way up there in the upper echelons where they made decisions. And this man moved among them with great dignity. The other members of the Sanhedrin—those men thought they knew him, but they did not know him.

Down underneath all of that mask that he was wearing, he was just plain, little-old Nicky. And the Lord Jesus was going to deal with him as plain, little-old Nicky—that's good psychologically, by the way. The head of the Psychology Department at the University of Southern California used to sit near the back of the auditorium on Thursday nights at the Bible study I was conducting. He used to correct me quite often on my psychology, but in regard to this portion of Scripture, he said, "You're right on target here. You are accurate about this man Nicodemus."

A great many people today function like that. They wear a mask to church and you don't really get acquainted with them. You don't really know who they are.

For example, here's a businessman today: He comes to his office on a morning and the staff that works for him gets busy all of a sudden. They had been loafing, but now the boss has come and they get busy. One of them turns to the new member of the staff and says, "That's Mr. Jones." "Oh, that's the boss?" "Yes." The secretary says to the boss, "There's a man waiting to see you." When she shows him in, this man says, "Mr. Jones, I've come to talk to you about a business deal and, by the way, how's business?" Mr. Jones says, "Oh, business is great! Everything is fine." And he's very dignified at the office there.

But at noon he goes to the club, and when he goes in, he's not Mr. Jones, the boss. They say to him, "Hello, Bill," and he says, "Hello, Jim." They pat each other on the back, and Jim asks, "How is business doing?" He says, "Oh, business is great."

But that evening he goes back home. He drives up in his big Cadillac, gets out, walks in, closes the door, and drops down in a chair. His wife comes over, puts her arm around him and asks, "What's the matter, Bill? Is business bad?" He says, "It's lousy."

And you say, that man is a hypocrite! No, he's not. That's the way he functions: he is a businessman, he is a member of the club, but he is also a husband at home, and I doubt that even his wife really knows him.

But Nicodemus, he was a man of the Pharisees, and he wore that mask. He was a ruler of the Jews, and he wore that mask. But down underneath he was plain little-old Nicky, and the Lord Jesus was going to deal with plain, little-old Nicky, not with a man of the Pharisees, not with a ruler of the Jews, and not with Mr. Businessman, either. My friend, the Lord Jesus will deal with you just as you are. That's the only way you can come to Him. "He had no need that anyone should testify of man." He knows what is in man. He knows who you are. Don't put up a front with Him.

I used to put up a front in prayer by trying to kid the Lord. I told Him one time I needed a new automobile so I could do better pastoral work, but really I'd met a new girl, and that was the reason I wanted the new car. I never told the Lord that, but He knew it and He let me have the car anyway!

Now as this man comes, you watch him approach the Lord Jesus. "This man came to Jesus by night." Now don't find fault with Nicodemus for coming by night. That was the best time to come. He was a busy man, and Jesus was very busy. Nighttime was when Nicodemus should come.

If you're going to find fault with him for coming at night, then why not find fault with the Lord's Supper? It was not established at an eleven o'clock morning service. It was established, I guess, around midnight. When in Israel, I always have gone down the pathway the Lord Jesus took on that last night. The Upper Room that is there now is not the real one, but the eleventh century one. But there was a room in that vicinity, and it was upstairs. Near midnight Jesus established the Lord's Supper there. It wasn't established in a church. These people today who say, "Oh, you've got to have communion in a church." Well, they should have been in Jerusalem to tell the Lord that, because He didn't know it. He used an upper room and it was night.

So this man Nicodemus came at night:

This man came to Jesus by night and said to Him, "Rabbi [teacher]**, we know that You are a teacher come from God; for no one can do these signs that You do unless God is with him."**
(John 3:2)

Now, there's something in that statement which is so tremendous! The first thing I mention is this: Did you know that the enemy never did question the miracles of Jesus? Nicodemus represented the Pharisees, the enemy, although they were friendly at the beginning. He was saying that the Pharisees recognized that He was performing miracles, and not just a few. We have a record of a few miracles in the Gospels, but when you read the Gospels, notice statements like this: He healed the *multitudes*.

Someone has asked the question: When He made His headquarters in Capernaum, why did He heal so many people there? Well, I found at least a partial answer to that question when we were in Tiberias. It's a lovely place. It wasn't in existence in Christ's day. The cities that were in existence in His day, He pronounced a judgment on them and they are gone. Tiberias is a new place, and right down from Tiberias are the springs to which people still come from everywhere because of their therapeutic value. So we can conclude that many sick people were in that area when Jesus was there. He didn't heal two or three blind men or two or three crippled men, He healed several *thousands* of them. Multitudes came to Him and He healed them. There was no question about His healing. There *is* a question about healing today, but there is no question about the healing done by the Lord Jesus. He *healed*. The enemy admitted that. They never charged that He did not heal people.

When Nicodemus came to Jesus that night he was sincere. He said, "We know." Who is "we"? We Pharisees. They had a meeting, I think, and Nicodemus was appointed the leader—"Brother Nicodemus, you go see Him. You meet with Him."

So Nicodemus met with Him that night, and he began by saying, "We know that You are a teacher come from God; for no one can do these signs that You do unless God is with him." That was flattery, but it was genuine flattery. If he had been wrong, our Lord would have corrected Him. Later on when the disciples of the Pharisees came, He said, "You hypocrites, who warned you to come?" He didn't say that to Nicodemus, for Nicodemus was genuine. But I'll say this, the Lord will take off his mask.

Listen to Him now as He answers Nicodemus.

Jesus answered and said to him, "Most assuredly, I say to you, unless one is born again, he cannot see the kingdom of God."
(John 3:3)

After Nicodemus had said, "No man can do these signs that You do unless God is with him," Jesus answered, "Most assuredly, I say to you, unless one is born *again*. . . ." I'd like to change the word *again* because it has gotten worn out and has practically lost its meaning. In the original, "again" is *anothan*, a Greek word which literally means "from above." Though the word also can be translated "again," what it means is "from above." He says here, "Unless one is born from above, he cannot see the kingdom of God."

Why did He mention the kingdom of God? Because Nicodemus wanted to talk about that. Now, I don't know about this, but I have a notion the Pharisees had talked it over: "Look, a new prophet has come down from the north, from Galilee. The people are following Him. He is performing miracles. Now if we can just hitch our wagon to His star, we could go places. Somebody should go and talk to Him because He's from up in the country and He doesn't know how to manipulate the politicians as we people down here do." And so it seems that Nicodemus came to the Lord Jesus with that proposition. And the Lord Jesus called his hand immediately. He lifted the mask of "a man of the Pharisees" from that man's face by saying to him, "Except a man be born from above he cannot even see the kingdom of God," and Nicodemus had wanted to talk about that.

Now notice that Nicodemus had another mask. He put it on in a hurry:

Nicodemus said to Him, "How can a man be born when he is old? Can he enter a second time into his mother's womb and be born?"
(John 3:4)

He missed it entirely, but you can see that he was now the ruler of the Jews. It is as if he was saying to the Lord Jesus: "What are You talking to me about? Are You trying to tell me something *new?* Don't You know that I'm a ruler of the Jews? If anything is known about this, I would know about it. How can this thing be? It's ridiculous, this thing that You're talking about."

Now the Lord Jesus is going to take off the second mask. Will you notice:

Jesus answered, "Most assuredly, I say to you, unless one is born of water and the Spirit, he cannot enter the kingdom of God."
(John 3:5)

Nicodemus, you need to be born again. You need to be born from *above*, or you can't even discuss this matter of the kingdom of God because you know nothing about it. Here the Lord Jesus strips off the other mask.

Now there has always been a question of what the

Lord Jesus meant by "born of water." There are those who feel that "water" is simply water baptism. I am confident He did not mean that at all, because at this stage He's not using water in that connection, and later in His ministry we read that the Lord Jesus never baptized. So evidently He means something else here. A further question is, what does He mean by "be born of water and of the Spirit"?

Well, I believe the water here refers to the Word of God. If you go over a little bit farther to John 7:37–38, you will find out that, during that great final day of the Feast of Tabernacles, they brought up water from the pool of Siloam and poured it out over the temple floor. I believe that the Lord Jesus stood in the temple that day and cried out,

"If anyone thirsts, let him come to Me and drink. He who believes in Me, as the Scripture has said, out of his heart will flow rivers of living water."

Then John hastens to add that He was speaking of the Holy Spirit. So, the Holy Spirit and the Word of God are tied together. Speaking of the church, the apostle Paul wrote that the Lord Jesus "gave Himself for her, that He might sanctify and cleanse her with the washing of water by the word" (Ephesians 5:25, 26). And we find in John 15:3, "You are already clean because of the word which I have spoken to you." The best bar of soap is not Ivory, it is this Bible. It has cleansing power. And when the Holy Spirit takes the Word of God and applies it to an individual who is a lost sinner, then that lost sinner can become a son of God through faith in the Lord Jesus Christ. And that, my friend, is the work of the Holy Spirit using the Word of God.

I do not believe that you can be saved through sentimental songs or sentimental talks. The only thing that can save a sinner is the Spirit of God using the *Word* of God. That is exactly what the Lord Jesus was talking to Nicodemus about. At least He had taken off the mask of the ruler of the Jews.

The Lord Jesus, though, went on. He said,

"That which is born of the flesh is flesh, and that which is born of the Spirit is spirit."
(John 3:6)

What He is doing here is putting down a tremendous principle of why the new birth is necessary, why you must be born from above. It's because that which is born of the flesh, it's flesh. We can do wonders with the flesh. We can improve it. When I was born, I didn't know A from B. They sent me to school and I found out that there's more than A and B. Education was very wonderful.

Then, I didn't have any manners. I used to run into the house when my mother would have company and I'd have my cap on. My mother would say, "Son, take your cap off. You're in the house and we have company." So I took my cap off. I had to be taught that, you know. I still to this good day, when I'm wearing a hat, if I get on an elevator and if there are women there, I take my hat off. I did it in London one day. I just took my hat off, and a man standing next to me looked at me for a minute or two, then he took his hat off. But when I got on an elevator right here in Los Angeles and I took my hat off, there were two women in there talking, and I found out they were Women's Libbers, so I put my hat back on. Oh, the flesh can be taught so many things. We had in Nashville, Tennessee, a school that taught girls how to hold a tea cup. You'd be surprised how important that little finger is in holding a tea cup! That's all manners. We have to be taught those things.

But, friends, after you've educated the flesh, after you've taught it manners, it's still *flesh*. You can give it all of this psychological self-esteem gospel that's being promulgated today, and when you get through with it you've got some nice polite individuals, but not one has been born from above. The Spirit of God has to produce a new nature. The Holy Spirit is not improving the old nature at all, although the old nature could stand a whole lot of improving.

Now will you notice Nicodemus. The Lord Jesus has stripped him of his mask and he stands there. He's really poor, little-old Nicky now. The Lord Jesus continues,

"Do not marvel that I said to you, 'You must be born again.' The wind blows where it wishes, and you hear the sound of it, but cannot tell where it comes from and where it goes. So is everyone who is born of the Spirit."
(John 3:7, 8)

Even the weatherman we listen to on the radio and
TV misses it sometimes. Oh, how he missed it the
other day. He said we were going to have an off-shore
wind, and it was an on-shore wind for a week. He
admitted that he had missed it. The wind blows where
it wills, we don't know where it comes from or where
it goes, but it comes from somewhere and it must go
somewhere, but, said the Lord Jesus, you don't know
where.

And now Nicodemus was ready to hear:

**Nicodemus answered and said to Him,
"How can these things be?"**
(John 3:9)

Isn't that wonderful? This was the man who knew
everything—"We know," he had said. Oh, these conceited people today! God can't save you, friends, if you
are in the "we know" crowd. But now Nicky was ready
to hear—"How can these things be?" So Jesus answered,
with gentle sarcasm,

**"Are you the teacher of Israel, and do not
know these things?"**
(John 3:10)

In other words, "Where's that mask you had on a while
ago when you knew everything? What about that?"

The Lord Jesus was going to speak to him very
clearly, and I'm going to drop down to verse 14:

"And as Moses lifted up the serpent in the

wilderness, even so must the Son of Man be lifted up."

Nicodemus knew what He was talking about because he knew that in the Old Testament God had sent fiery serpents. He knew that God had directed Moses to make a bronze serpent to represent the sins of the people and to lift it up on a pole. All that the people had to do was *look* to live, and now He said to him, "Just as Moses lifted up the serpent, I'm going to be lifted up. I who knew no sin will be made sin for you in order that you might be saved."

Now notice the following verses:

"That whoever believes in Him should not perish but have eternal life. For God so loved the world that He gave His only begotten Son. . . ."
(John 3:15, 16)

God loved the *whole world*. I don't know what you "election boys" do with that verse, but it is in the Word of God. Anyone can be saved who will turn to Jesus. He is the propitiation for the sins of the whole world, the *whole world*.

On my last tour to Israel I stood looking up at Gordon's Calvary, the site we accept as being the place of our Lord's crucifixion. His agony, His crucifixion, His burial—all took place in an area the size of a football field. He was crucified up there, and down below there is the empty tomb, not far apart. You can stand in the same place and see both locations. I told our tour group, which was standing there with me, "Our salvation was wrought out in this geographical place. He did it here for you and for me."

Today there is a busy bus station on the street below that bluff which we call Calvary. While I was standing there at the corner, a crowd came up to go across the street, and an Arab boy lifted up my shirt and started to put his hand in where my billfold was. He got his hand into the pocket, but he didn't get the billfold. I whirled on him, and I called him a thief. He walked across the street, and in a few minutes a taxi came by. There were several boys who climbed in and began to take out of their pockets what they had stolen. I had called that young fellow a thief, and I would have given anything in the world if I could have gone over to him and said, "Look, right up there a Man died on a cross between two thieves. He saved one of them, and He can save you." But I couldn't speak Arabic, and he couldn't understand English. We have an Arabic radio broadcast which reaches that area; I hope he hears about the Man who died up there between two thieves—died for *him,* if you please. "God so loved the world, that He gave his only begotten Son, that whoever. . . ." *Whoever*—that's Vernon McGee and that Arab boy and that's you—"whoever believes in Him should not perish but have everlasting life."

Did Nicodemus ever make a decision for Christ? Well, the Bible doesn't tell us, but it does give us some clues. When the chief priests and the Pharisees wanted Jesus arrested, the officers returned to them empty-handed.

Then the officers came to the chief priests

and Pharisees, who said to them, "Why
have you not brought Him?" The officers
answered, "No man ever spoke like this
Man!"
(John 7:45, 46)

Then the Pharisees ridiculed the officers for being deceived and said,

"Are you also deceived? Have any of the
rulers or the Pharisees believed in Him?
But this crowd that does not know the law
is accursed."
(John 7:47–49)

Listen to Nicodemus as he spoke up:

Nicodemus (he who came to Jesus by night,
being one of them) said to them, "Does our
law judge a man before it hears him and
knows what he is doing?"
(John 7:50, 51)

Now, I admit that's a weak defense, but it *is* a defense
for the Lord Jesus that he put up even before the
powerful Sanhedrin.

Another clue that Nicodemus became a believer
was the day when the Lord Jesus was crucified and,
I say this reverently, Joseph of Arimathea and
Nicodemus served as the undertakers to handle the
body.

After this, Joseph of Arimathea, being a

disciple of Jesus, but secretly, for fear of the Jews, asked Pilate that he might take away the body of Jesus; and Pilate gave him permission. So he came and took the body of Jesus. And Nicodemus, who at first came to Jesus by night, also came, bringing a mixture of myrrh and aloes, about a hundred pounds.
(John 19:38, 39)

I suppose those two men, Joseph and Nicodemus, worked two or three hours. They would have first anointed the body with costly oil, then wrapped it with linen strips and sealed them with spices like a mummy. Each finger would have been wrapped separately, then the hand, the arm, and the whole body. This is the reason that, on the morning of the resurrection when John looked into the tomb and saw all those stiffened linen wrappings undisturbed and the body gone, he knew that the Lord Jesus Christ had risen from the dead.

When I was in Israel I looked into that tomb again and thought of those two men in there working on the body of Jesus. When they came to those awful wounds that He had—the body of Jesus was so bloody—and when they saw that spear wound in His side, I think probably Nicodemus said, "Joseph, I remember the night three years ago when He told me, 'As Moses lifted up the serpent in the wilderness, even so must the Son of Man be lifted up.' And then He went on to say, 'God so loved the world that He gave His only begotten Son, that whoever believes in Him. . . .'" And I think Nicodemus said,

"Joseph,I *believe* in Him." I feel this man Nicodemus came to faith in the Lord.

My friend, like Nicodemus believed and Joseph of Arimathea believed, you have the opportunity to trust the Lord Jesus Christ as your Savior and become a child of God through faith in Christ.

— 9 —

STEPHEN AND SAUL
The Martyr and the Murderer

The two men who constitute our subject, Stephen and Saul (later called Paul), had this in common: They were both young men—that is, they were young men when they first met. It is not altogether inaccurate to state that the early church was a youth movement. Both Stephen and Saul gave to the church their very lives. Both had a great deal to do with shaping the course of the church on the human plane. Both were remarkable young men. Both of them were gifted by the Holy Spirit. But the only time the two ever met, they were bitter enemies.

Actually, Saul hated Stephen. Each of them stood on opposite sides of the cross. The cross divided these two young men, as truly as it did the two thieves who were crucified at the same time our Lord died—one at His right and one at His left. Saul of Tarsus later wrote in

1 Corinthians 1:18, "For the message of the cross is foolishness to those who are perishing." And at the time when he and Stephen met, the cross to him was indeed foolishness. Then Paul went on to say, "but to us who are being saved it is the power [the dynamite (*dunamis*) power] of God." And that had been the experience of Stephen when they met.

STEPHEN'S STORY

Now Stephen's story comes before us first in Scripture in Acts chapters 6 and 7 where we read that the early church was already having difficulty, and the difficulty was that there were two groups of believers. One group was Hebrew; the other folk, in addition to being Hebrew, were also Hellenists—Greeks, as our King James translation has it, which simply means that they were Hebrews who were born outside of Palestine and spoke the Greek language. That was their culture, just as today Jews born in America are Americans and speak English. These people were Greek in that sense, although they were Jews. They felt their widows were being neglected in the distribution of food, and since the apostles did not have time to supervise this, here is what happened:

> **Then the twelve summoned the multitude of the disciples and said, "It is not desirable that we should leave the word of God and serve tables. Therefore, brethren, seek out from among you seven men of good reputation, full of the Holy Spirit and wisdom, whom we may appoint over this business."** (Acts 6:2, 3)

So these seven men were to be chosen as deacons, for the word *servant* here is the word "deacon," and it is where we get our title *deacon* for officers in our churches.

Now the office of deacon at this time did not have prominence, certainly not in the early church as it does today in many of our churches. In other words, today the office of deacon is held by those who have responsibility for the spiritual welfare of the church. That was never true in the early church at all. They were never in a place of authority. They were servants in the early church, and the thing that marked them was their humility. So that is how the office of deacon came into view, and this was the first organization that appeared in the local church.

Actually, very little information, only shreds and sketches, is given of any organization in the early church. The Holy Spirit was working in the church, and Christ was the Head of the church. That He was the authority was kept before them constantly.

Now these men who were to be chosen were men who had to have certain requirements, and Stephen was the first one who was called to our attention. He was actually separated from the others. We are told:

And the saying pleased the whole multitude. And they chose Stephen, a man full of faith and the Holy Spirit. . . .
(Acts 6:5)

The name *Stephen* means "crown." It is a Greek name. He was a Hellenist, and it is interesting that all of the deacons who were chosen were Hellenists. Wasn't that a lovely thing that the early church did? I'll tell you how we would do it today: We would say, "Well, you have to choose half of the deacons from one side and half from the other side in order to make it fair!" The early church said, "No, these Hellenists feel like they haven't been treated fairly, so we will put all Hellenists on the Board of Deacons." And that is the way they did it. It was a very gracious move on the part of the early church, under the supervision of the Holy Spirit of course.

Now Stephen's name, meaning *crown*, is certainly an appropriate name for this man who was the first one crowned a martyr of the church. I daresay that when his mother named him, she never dreamed that he would be the first martyr for Christ.

A Man of Faith

We are told that Stephen was full of faith, which means more than saving faith. It is not the amount of faith that saves you; it is where your faith is placed. It is not even the condition of your faith. It may be even a fearful faith, but faith placed in Jesus Christ will save.

I travel by air when I have to, and some time ago I flew back to California all the way from Nashville, Tennessee. I didn't enjoy it, but I had enough faith to get a ticket and get on the plane. And I know that others fly with lots more faith than I have, but I want to say this: they don't go any faster than I do, and I go the same way they do. I get there just exactly like they get there.

The important thing is where your faith is placed, whether it is in Christ or not. Spurgeon said, "It is not thy joy in Christ that saves thee, it is Christ; it is not thy hope in Christ that saves thee, it is Christ. It is not even thy faith in Christ, though that may be the instrument. It is Christ's blood and merit that saves." Faith merely attaches us to Him. Therefore it can be a very weak faith.

This man Stephen was a man full of faith, and that means that his life, as we shall see, was based on conviction, a conviction that came to him because he was also full of wisdom. The congregation was told to select men full of the Holy Spirit and wisdom, but when they picked Stephen we are told he was a man full of faith and the Holy Spirit. May I say to you, his faith was anchored on a real knowledge, and it was built on that which was common sense.

The president of a seminary in this country years ago said to a young man who came to him, "When you come here, there are three things that you will need. You'll need grit, and you'll need gifts, and you'll need gumption." Gumption is one of the most important things, and that's what this man Stephen had—it means sanctified common sense. That was the requirement of the deacon, if you please. He was full of wisdom, and it gave this man a conviction, a remarkable conviction, so that it is said of him in verse 10, "And they [his enemies] were not able to resist the wisdom and the Spirit by which he spoke."

These folk in our day who are wobbly in their faith are not much of a witness for Christ. Those who think that they can adopt the latest fad or run with both the hare and the hounds do not win souls for Christ. This man Stephen had a conviction! *Conviction* comes from the same word from which we get our word *convict*, and believe me, a convict is a fellow who has been convicted.

We need, today, believers who are convicts—convicts in the sense they are convicted, men full of faith. And that was the thing that marked this man Stephen.

Full of the Spirit

Then we are told that Stephen was full of the Holy Spirit. Five times it is mentioned in the record concerning Stephen that he was full of the Holy Spirit. But what is the mark of a Spirit-filled man? Have you ever stopped to think how you would make an identification of a Spirit-filled man? Well, first of all, he would have to be a man who had the fruit of the Spirit in his life. "But the fruit of the Spirit is love, joy, peace, longsuffering, kindness, goodness, faithfulness, gentleness, self-control." (Galatians 5:22, 23). All those wonderful graces should be in his life, that is true, but it is also interesting to note that when Paul, in the Epistle to the Ephesians, talks about being filled with the Spirit, he brings it right down to earth and puts it in shoe leather.

Notice how he lets it walk. He says, "And do not be drunk with wine, in which is dissipation; but be filled with the Spirit" (Ephesians 5:18). And then he says, "Submitting to one another in the fear of God" (Ephesians 5:21). That's a Spirit-filled man, one willing to submit to others.

And it goes into the home, "Wives, submit to your own husbands, as to the Lord" (Ephesians 5:22). He's talking about a Spirit-filled wife here. And he talks about Spirit-filled husbands: "Husbands, love your wives, just as Christ' also loved the church and gave Himself for her" (Ephesians 5:25). You see, a deacon was to be a Spirit-filled man, and a Spirit-filled man has a home where he loves his wife, and his wife loves him and submits to him. You see, this is practical. My friend, if Christianity is not practical, it is not worth anything. If it doesn't walk in shoe leather, you can dismiss it.

And Paul is not through with that. He takes it further into the home: "Children, obey your parents in the Lord, for this is right" (Ephesians 6:1). A saved young person will be obedient to the parents. If he is not, he is not a Spirit-filled Christian, you can be sure of that. And Paul also says, "And you, fathers, do not provoke your children to wrath, but bring them up in the training and admonition of the Lord" (Ephesians 6:4). A Spirit-filled father will not get angry and beat a child under the impulse of the moment. He will discipline, but not through his temper.

Being filled with the Spirit also works itself out in the business world. It will go to work on Monday morning: "Bondservants, be obedient to those who are your masters. . . . And you, masters, do the same things to them. . . ." (Ephesians 6:5, 9). My, if big business only had a few more Spirit-filled executives and Spirit-filled employees and Spirit-filled labor leaders, it would have some of its knotty problems settled before morning!

May I say to you that this lifestyle is the mark of being a Spirit-filled person. This thing is practical. My friend, you do not go into orbit living the Christian life; you walk on solid earth. The Christian life is not an occasional flight into space; it is a day-by-day walk down the streets of our cities, in our neighborhoods, in our places of business, in our homes. And that is the kind of man Stephen was—a man who walked Roman roads in a pagan society and lived for God. That is the man we're talking about.

> **And Stephen, full of faith and power, did great wonders and signs among the people. Then there arose some from what is called the Synagogue of the Freedmen (Cyrenians, Alexandrians, and those from Cilicia and Asia), disputing with Stephen. And they were not able to resist the wisdom and the Spirit by which he spoke. Then they secretly induced men to say, "We have heard him speak blasphemous words against Moses and God." And they stirred up the people, the elders, and the scribes; and they came upon him, seized him, and brought him to the council.**
> (Acts 6:8–12)

Now this man was brought to trial because, as he was witnessing concerning Christ, these antagonists could not answer him. The council he was brought before was the *Sanhedrin* (the Greek word for a council), the same group that had condemned the Lord Jesus to death. False charges were brought against Stephen as they had been brought against our Lord.

> **They also set up false witnesses who said, "This man does not cease to speak blasphemous words against this holy place and the law; for we have heard him say that this Jesus of Nazareth will destroy this place**

and change the customs which Moses delivered to us."
(Acts 6:13, 14)

Putting it in the colloquialism of the police department, he was framed.

Stephen's defense is a long catalog of the history of the nation Israel from Abraham down to the crucifixion. It is the longest chapter in the Book of Acts, and actually one of the most important. In this Stephen is not at all defending himself. He is bringing a charge against his nation. He goes over their history, and it is actually the Holy Spirit's interpretation of the Old Testament. When Stephen went before the Sanhedrin, he began where any Jew would begin. He began with Abraham, and he told how God called Abraham and how Abraham walked with God by faith. And then he takes up two men, Joseph and Moses. Why did he use Joseph and Moses for an illustration? All you have to do is read it, and you'll find out why. Oh, this crowd that heard him didn't miss the point, and let us not miss the point either. Stephen says to them that Joseph was sold by his brethren. There are those who say that Joseph is one of the finest pictures of Christ that we have in the Old Testament but that he is never mentioned in the New Testament. May I say to you that he *is* mentioned in the New Testament. Stephen is the one who talked about him a great deal, and this is the thing that he said: Joseph was disowned by his own brethren. They sold him into slavery, but God had determined that he was to be their deliverer, and Joseph actually saved the nation.

The council didn't miss the point. They knew that the

One Stephen was referring to was Jesus—that Jesus had come, had been betrayed by the nation to the Roman Empire, and had been crucified on a Roman cross, but that even then He was their Redeemer and would save them if they would but turn to Him. And you find at this time, if you read the record carefully, that a great company of priests turned to God—they heard Stephen and they got the message! Joseph was like the Lord Jesus in that he delivered his brethren though they had disowned him, and this is what Stephen was telling his nation.

He also spoke of Moses. He said that Moses came as a redeemer and as a savior in his day. Although Moses had even killed an Egyptian slavemaster who was persecuting one of his brethren, the people of Israel would not accept him. They actually repudiated him when he wanted to help them, and he had to flee down into the land of Midian. Forty years later, God brought him back to Egypt, and Moses returned as their deliverer. At first they still did not want him. In fact, the very organization that Stephen was talking to—the Sanhedrin of Moses' day, the elders of the people—was the same one to whom Moses came, and at first they would not accept him. But despite their initial rejection he became their redeemer, and he delivered them out of slavery.

The Sanhedrin didn't miss Stephen's point. They knew that what he meant was this: The rebellious heart in that nation in its infancy, which had first rejected Joseph and then when grown to maturation had rejected Moses, had now in full-grown manhood repudiated and rejected their Redeemer, the Lord Jesus Christ.

It is the same thing that is in the hearts of men and women in our world today when they turn their backs on Jesus Christ. It is still that same rebellion in the human heart which rejects Him and makes people hate Him. The Sanhedrin hated Christ, and they hated Stephen because he was witnessing to them of Him.

May I say to you that Acts 7 is God's interpretation of Israel's history. I'd love to see God's interpretation of the history of the church, wouldn't you? I want to read it because I do think that He has recorded the history of the church, and it would be something like Israel's history. Someday I think we'll get to see it. The same rebellion has come down for nearly two thousand years. The story of the church, as one church historian has said, is the story of heresy—rebellion in the human heart.

As you can see, Stephen was not defending himself, he was leveling charges against them.

> **"You stiff-necked and uncircumcised in heart and ears! You always resist the Holy Spirit; as your fathers did, so do you."**
> (Acts 7:51).

But he got no further than right here, when they stopped him dead in his tracks. Notice their reaction as he came to the end of his message:

> **When they heard these things they were cut to the heart, and they gnashed at him with their teeth.**
> (Acts 7:54)

When men have no argument, they become angry and act like this.

Now will you notice what happened:

But he, being full of the Holy Spirit, gazed into heaven and saw the glory of God, and Jesus standing at the right hand of God, and said, "Look! I see the heavens opened and the Son of Man standing at the right hand of God!"
(Acts 7:55, 56)

The thing that will interest anyone who reads this carefully is our Lord Himself. What is the Lord Jesus doing standing? Not that we're arguing about a posture, but it is interesting to note that all of the Scripture, even Dr. Luke in his Gospel, says that when Jesus went back to heaven He then sat down at the right hand of God. The writer to the Hebrews says,

Looking unto Jesus, the author and finisher of our faith, who for the joy that was set before Him endured the cross, despising the shame, and has sat down at the right hand of the throne of God.
(Hebrews 12:2)

That He sat down is emphasized because redemption is a finished transaction. Our Lord didn't have to get up and go do something else in order to redeem us.

If you imagine that our Lord is just sitting there today, I think you are wrong. Stephen saw Him standing. Why was He standing? Well, because in a little while He was going to say to the man who hated Him more than anyone else, "Saul, Saul, why are you persecuting Me?" And Saul, whom we also know as the apostle Paul, said later on that if one member of the body suffers, all suffer with it. Christ is the Head of the body; you cannot, my friend, attempt to harm a member of the body of Christ without making Jesus Christ hurt. That is something for you to think over the next time you want to do something against a member of the body of Christ. You will hurt Jesus Christ. If one member suffers, all members suffer. He was standing up. Why? Because this man Stephen was going to be His first martyr, and He was standing to receive him, if you please.

SAUL'S STORY

I want to leave that for a moment and ask this question: How did Dr. Luke know so much about the trial of Stephen? "Oh," somebody says, "the Holy Spirit called all those things to his mind." Right, that is true. But you know, God also uses the human element in Scripture. Dr. Luke had a personal friend who had been there. He was the young Pharisee, a member of the Council of Sanhedrin, who hated Jesus Christ and His followers more than all of them. When the rest of the enemies of Christ drove the believers out of Jerusalem, the Sanhedrin sat back, satisfied. But not this young man. He was going to drive them out of Damascus, and he didn't intend to stop there. He would ferret the Christians out anywhere he found them all over the Roman Empire. He had been present at the trial of Stephen.

That young Pharisee was named Saul of Tarsus. He saw Stephen's face shine like that of an angel. I think it made quite an impression on him. He heard Stephen cry, "Look! I see the heavens opened, and the Son of Man standing at the right hand of God!" And that fellow Saul was skeptical, cynical, but I think he looked up wistfully, longingly, anxiously. Oh, if he could only see heaven open!

Why should Saul look up? Why should he? He was superior to Stephen. What did Stephen have that he didn't have? Outwardly, he was way out yonder and above this man Stephen in every department of life. Put that proud Pharisee down by the side of that humble deacon, and the proud young Pharisee had everything that the world counts worthwhile. Positionally, Saul was far above and removed from the humble deacon in the lowly church built by the Carpenter of Nazareth.

Legally Righteous

Now let's look at Saul for a moment. We know a great deal about him, lots more about him than about any of the other apostles. He was an Israelite, and he was of pure blood. He certainly emphasized that:

For I also am an Israelite, of the seed of Abraham, of the tribe of Benjamin.
(Romans 11:1)

Paul said that of himself, and it would have been with pride back in the days of his flesh. That had meant a great deal to him as a young Pharisee. He said, "I belong to the tribe of Benjamin." Benjamin became the favorite son of old Jacob, the last son born of his beautiful wife Rachel. The tribe of Benjamin was placed next to Judah in importance. It was the tribe that Saul, Israel's first king, had come from (see 1 Samuel 9).

And in his flesh, Paul had even more to be proud of. He says,

Though I also might have confidence in the flesh. If anyone else thinks he may have confidence in the flesh, I more so: circumcised the eighth day, of the stock of Israel, of the tribe of Benjamin, a Hebrew of the Hebrews; concerning the law, a Pharisee; concerning zeal, persecuting the church; concerning the righteousness which is in the law, blameless.
(Philippians 3:4–6)

He said, "I was circumcised the eighth day." That's just like people would say today, "I've been baptized," or "I'm a Presbyterian," or "I'm a Methodist," or "I'm a Baptist." God forgive us for taking pride in those things. That is baby talk to begin with, but nevertheless that's what he was saying, "I was circumcised the eighth day. I have background."

He was a Roman citizen by birth. That was worth a great deal in that day. That gave him entree everywhere. His Roman citizenship gave him access yonder into Caesar's palace. Our Lord had said of Paul when he was converted, "He is a chosen vessel of Mine to bear My name before Gentiles, kings, and the children of Israel" (Acts 9:15). "I'll have him appear before kings," and He did. Paul was a Roman citizen.

He was born in Tarsus, and when he was giving his defense, he said, "I am a Jew from Tarsus, in Cilicia, a citizen of no mean city" (Acts 21:39). And the reason it was no mean city, that is, not lacking in distinction, is because there was a Greek university there. In that day, the best of all universities was at Tarsus. I do not know this, but I imagine that Paul was a graduate, probably had his master's degree from that university.

He knew Greek philosophy, he knew Greek culture, and he was also a Pharisee. He said,

"I am indeed a Jew, born in Tarsus of Cilicia, but brought up in this city at the feet of Gamaliel, taught according to the strictness of our fathers' law, and was zealous toward God as you all are today."
(Acts 22:3)

He was a Hebrew of the Hebrews. He sat at the feet of Gamaliel, the greatest Hebrew teacher, and now he was a young Pharisee—probably the youngest. He was brilliant, most likely had the highest IQ of any man that the church has ever had. I'm confident he stands above these so-called intellectuals of our day.

Saul's Sin

Paul had been a Pharisee. He was firm on the fundamentals of the Jewish faith. Concerning his relationship to the Law, he said, "I was blameless." That doesn't mean he was perfect. Don't get that impression, because he was not perfect. When he says he was blameless, he means he brought all the sacrifices required by the Law. This man had sinned, and he confesses that fact in the seventh chapter of Romans. When he put the Ten Commandments down on his life and he found out where he had failed, he said,

> **What shall we say then? Is the law sin? Certainly not! On the contrary, I would not have known sin except through the law. For I would not have known covetousness unless the law had said, "You shall not covet."**
> (Romans 7:7)

Covetousness is the nice respectable sin you can commit today. "Oh, I wish I had that automobile. I wish I lived in that home." And ladies, window shopping can put you on the highest plane of the sin of covetousness. The preacher in the pulpit can be coveting and nobody will be the wiser. And Paul could put nine of the Ten Commandments down on his life and say, "I keep those." I daresay there's not anyone reading this message who can stand up and say, "I keep nine of the Ten Commandments." If Paul had kept his mouth shut, we would have thought he was perfect, but he added, "This tenth one got me." What did he do when it got him, when he realized coveting was sin? He recognized he was a sinner. And he said, "According to the Law I am blameless," which means he brought the prescribed sacrifice. But although Paul brought that sacrifice, it never did satisfy his heart. He hated the believers in the Lord Jesus Christ because he was a proud and arrogant, ambitious young man.

Saul's Great Need

Down underneath that exterior, though, there was a

deep dissatisfaction and discontent. He had a great need. He was not sure of his salvation. He did not know whether he was rightly related to God at all. And when he listened to Stephen, he knew that Stephen had something that he, Saul of Tarsus, did not have. He looked in unbelief at the heavens, and, in bitterness and hatred against Jesus Christ, I think he might have said, "Stephen says he sees Jesus. I don't see Him, and if I saw Him I would be willing to crucify Him again!" And I think Saul had been there with the first crowd that had crucified our Lord. I don't think that brilliant young Pharisee who hated Him stayed home on the big day when they did at last crucify Him. Saul must have been there.

In Saul's heart there was a void and a vacuum and a growing hunger. He had a need, but that didn't keep him from condemning this man Stephen. The very interesting thing is that immediately after Stephen said he saw heaven opened and Jesus standing there,

Then they cried out with a loud voice, stopped their ears, and ran at him with one accord; and they cast him out of the city and stoned him. And the witnesses laid down their clothes at the feet of a young man named Saul.
(Acts 7:57, 58)

Stephen was condemned, and the executioner was Saul of Tarsus. He liked the job. To put it in more current terms, he pulled the switch on the electric chair, or he pulled the trip for the hangman's noose, or he is the one who dropped the pellets into the gas chamber. And he loved it when the victim happened to be a Christian.

> **And they stoned Stephen as he was calling on God and saying, "Lord Jesus, receive my spirit." Then he knelt down and cried out with a loud voice, "Lord, do not charge them with this sin." And when he had said this, he fell asleep.**
> (Acts 7:59, 60)

Death was not defeat for Stephen. "Lord Jesus, receive my spirit." He didn't die like the average man dies. Death to him was a victory. And then he did something else. He prayed for those who were stoning him, which included Saul. Stephen prayed for Saul! Then we're told "he fell asleep." What does this mean? It means that Jesus put his body to sleep to await the Rapture. The body that was mangled went to sleep, and he is, as Paul said later, "Absent from the body . . . present with the Lord" (2 Corinthians 5:8). What an entrance into heaven Stephen must have had! Jesus was standing up there waiting for him. He stood up to receive him. I wonder if He will stand up when you get there and when I get there. He did for Stephen.

Will you notice this, Stephen had asked the Lord to forgive his tormentors, and Saul stood there looking down at the battered and bloody body of this man, his skull probably crushed by a heavy stone after he had fallen. He was mangled. Then Saul looked up. I do not know this, but I think he sighed, "Oh, if I could only see heaven opened. If Jesus is alive, I want to know it." You say, "How do you know that went on in his mind?" Would you like to hear his testimony? When he was brought before Agrippa, the king, this is what he had to say:

"Why should it be thought incredible by you that God raises the dead? Indeed, I myself thought I must do many things contrary to the name of Jesus of Nazareth. This I also did in Jerusalem, and many of the saints I shut up in prison, having received authority from the chief priests; and when they were put to death, I cast my vote against them. And I punished them often in every synagogue and compelled them to blaspheme; and being exceedingly enraged against them, I persecuted them even to foreign cities."
(Acts 26:8–11)

May I say to you, Paul believed in the resurrection: "I'd love to see Him if He is alive."

Encountering Christ

Saul was on the way to Damascus. He had gotten papers of authority and commission from the chief priests to arrest Christians and to put them to death in Damascus. On the way it happened! The Lord Jesus appeared to this man—Saul saw heaven opened; he saw the resurrected Christ, the glorified Christ!

Only three men have seen Him in that state— Stephen, Saul, and John. Interesting. They are the only three. First, Stephen represents the church; that is, the body of true believers which will be caught up to be in

Christ's presence. Oh, in that day He will stand again to receive His church. Second, Saul represents that remnant of Israel which is to be saved during the Tribulation, and Christ will stand to receive His Tribulation saints. Third, the apostle John saw Christ and sets before us the judgment of God—when Christ comes in judgment to this earth. Christ's appearance to Saul on the Damascus Road was the experience which made him an apostle of Jesus Christ. Paul always went back to it. He said, "I have seen Him!"

Saul's conversion was one of three great conversions that are given to us in detail in the Book of Acts. First there is the conversion of the Ethiopian eunuch in chapter eight, then there is the conversion of Saul of Tarsus in chapter nine, and finally there is the conversion of Cornelius in chapter ten. These are representative of the three sons of Noah—a descendant of Ham, a descendant of Shem, and a descendant of Japheth.

You find that the glorified Savior used three means of bringing about their conversion. And I think He still uses the three means. I am convinced that the pattern has never been changed. First, He brings into one focal point the Spirit of God who is supervising it. Second, the Word of God is always used; there can't be a conversion apart from the Word of God, for we are told that men are "born again . . . through the word of God which lives and abides forever" (1 Peter 1:23). And third, He always uses a man of God. And when the Spirit of God takes the Word of God and uses a man of God, there is always a child of God who comes into existence. Always.

Now somebody's going to say, "Well, preacher, I think

you missed it with Saul, because on the Damascus Road there was no human instrumentality at all." You are correct, in that on the Damascus Road there was no human instrumentality, but there was an individual involved in the conversion of Saul of Tarsus. Come back with me to that place outside the walls of Jerusalem. A mob has just stoned a young man, and another young man stands there looking at him, bloody, battered, and beaten. That young man on the ground is Stephen. Five minutes before he had said, "I see the heavens opened, and Jesus standing. . . ." And he had asked Him to forgive them, to forgive even the young man who was consenting to his execution. This brilliant young Pharisee did not know what he was doing. And the Lord heard the prayer of Stephen. On the Damascus Road He waylaid Saul of Tarsus. Now I don't know anyone who has ever had a greater human instrument than the first martyr as his witness! God always uses the human factor in the equation of conversion.

May I tell this little story, and then I'm through. Some years ago there was a tragic explosion in a school in New London, Texas, which was on an East Texas oil field. Many years later I had lunch in Chicago with Dexter, who had been a young pastor in that field at the time. He went out as a seminary student, and then after he graduated he pastored his first church in that field.

This young pastor told of a man who had been nothing in the world but a farmer. But oil was discovered on his land, and this fellow developed real ability in handling his money. He even started his own refinery and became tremendously wealthy. The wealthier he became, the more blasphemous he became. He had a vile tongue.

During a flu epidemic, his wife and one of his two little boys took sick. Dexter said, "I went over to see them. They were not attending church because the father wouldn't let them." But earlier Dexter had had the privilege of leading the two boys to the Lord in a Bible school, and then had also reached the mother. Hearing that they were sick, he went to the door of this man's lavish colonial home and saw that he was living like a lord out there in East Texas on one of those red clay hills. The man shut the door in his face and would not permit him to come in.

Two days later the little boy and the mother died. Dexter thought, *Well, I can talk to him now.* But when he went over and walked in, the man began to abuse him. He called him everything under the sun, cursed him, and Dexter told me, "I couldn't do a thing in the world but just turn and walk out."

Dexter did conduct the funeral, but the man wasn't even listening to him. He had one little boy left, and he gave all of his love and attention to that child. And that little boy was in the New London School when it exploded.

When the father got there, driving like a madman in his big Cadillac, he tore through the debris, frantically digging it out with his bare hands. Finally, they did find the body of his little boy. The father took it up in his arms and in a daze paced up and down with it until the authorities had to take it from him.

Dexter made a point of visiting every family of the 300 children who were killed in that explosion. So he started going from home to home that night. He said, "When I went up to that great big southern home, I just braced myself for a cursing—I knew he would curse me.

When I rang the doorbell, a servant came and opened the door. I walked in, and sitting over there was the father beside the little boy's casket. I walked over and sat down. The father didn't say a word. I didn't do anything but get out my New Testament and start reading. I read to him, I guess, for thirty minutes, and I began to see tears coming down his cheeks. Finally, he interrupted me. He put his hand over on my knee and he said, 'Look, preacher, you don't have to talk to me. I've known all the time that God was after me, and He had to do this to get me. But now He's got me. I'll come to Christ.' And he did."

God always uses a human instrument, always. Oh, He will go about it in a very strange way sometimes, but when He is after a man or a woman, He uses a human instrument. And in the apostle Paul's case that instrument was Stephen, the church's first martyr.

— 10 —

AGRIPPA

The King Who Couldn't Decide

One kingly characteristic is the ability to make a quick, just, and right decision at the right time. The king is the one who should make the decision. It was said of Napoleon that his amazing ability as a military commander was to make a brilliant maneuver at a moment's notice and execute it speedily. That was the thing that made him a great man. He called himself a man of destiny, one who could make a decision.

Most assuredly, a king ought to be able to decide. That was one of the instructions Solomon's mother gave him in the last chapter of Proverbs. She told him that he should be able to make a decision justly and righteously:

Open your mouth, judge righteously, and plead the cause of the poor and needy.
(Proverbs 31:9)

He should be able to decide. This is an attribute that should characterize a king.

However, every person ought to be able to decide concerning the eternal destiny of his soul. All, from the prince in the palace to the pauper in the hovel, must be able to make a decision, and each *has* to make that decision. A rich young ruler came to Christ, and he made a wrong decision. The poor, sinful woman came to Christ in the home of the Pharisee, and she made the right decision.

Now the king before us, King Agrippa, had an opportunity to hear the most eloquent and persuasive preacher of the gospel of all times. He heard Paul the apostle. When the Lord Jesus had stopped Paul on the Damascus Road, actually waylaid him, and this man had yielded to Him, one of the things God said was that "he is a chosen vessel of Mine to bear My name before Gentiles, [and] kings. . . ." (Acts 9:15). And so Paul the apostle had the opportunity to bear the name of Christ before kings, and we see him here as he appeared before King Agrippa, for that is the king whose life we are looking at now.

Who is King Agrippa? Well, historically he was Agrippa II. He was a member of the Herod family, and I submit to you that this was one of the worst families that has ever appeared on the earth. They would outdo the house of Medici in Italy, and they would outdo any other rascals who have ever appeared on the pages of history. The Herods came out of the nation of Edom, and Edom came from the man Esau.

King Agrippa II was a great-grandson of Herod the Great, which made him the great-grandson of the man who had attempted to put Jesus to death when He was a baby. Agrippa also had a great-uncle who had put John the Baptist to death, and he had an uncle who put James the apostle to death. It seems like the Herod family got wrapped up in the gospel, and they put many of God's men to death. That is one reason God could say near the end of the Old Testament, "Jacob have I loved and Esau have I hated"—because the Herods were going to descend from Esau.

Although Agrippa II was an Edomite, he was the best of the Herod family. He came nearer to salvation than did any other member of the Herod family. He was educated in Rome. In fact, he spent a great deal of his youth in Rome. Caesar, who was his friend, made him the king over the land of Palestine—first when he was seventeen years old. Then when Caesar recognized that Agrippa was too young to be sent there, he kept him until he was twenty-one and then sent him back into Palestine.

This man Agrippa II, although a member of the Herod family, was a very remarkable man in many ways. He knew a great deal about the Jews' religion. He made it his business to know Jewish customs and to know the Old Testament. However, he never was a popular ruler among the Jews. Once, when the Jews were ready to revolt, they took to the streets, and Agrippa made an impassioned plea before them. He concluded it in tears, and the mob was so moved by it that they actually desisted, broke up, and went back to their homes. At that time they did not revolt against him. But finally, when they were aroused again and took to the streets, Agrippa joined the Roman soldiers under the general Titus who besieged Jerusalem. He fought against the Jews, and Jerusalem was destroyed.

That was in A.D. 70, and at that time the nation was scattered and was brought to an end. Never to this day have they recovered. Of course, in 1948 they were recognized as a nation, but they have not yet returned to their land in a way that would fulfill the prophecies of the Scriptures.

Agrippa had been a profligate; he was affected and infected by the immorality of the Roman Empire at that time. His marriage to Bernice was a sordid scandal. She was his own sister. She had been married twice before and apparently poisoned one husband. At least she knew how to get rid of them.

You can imagine Paul the apostle standing before this couple, Agrippa and Bernice, presenting the gospel to them! Agrippa heard the gospel, for after Paul had been arrested he appeared before this man for his judgment of the case. Let's get our background by turning to Acts 25:13–27:

And after some days King Agrippa and Bernice came to Caesarea to greet Festus.

Then dropping down to verse 24:

And Festus said: "King Agrippa and all the men who are here present with us, you see

this man about whom the whole assembly of the Jews petitioned me, both at Jerusalem and here, crying out that he was not fit to live any longer. But when I found that he had committed nothing deserving of death, and that he himself had appealed to Augustus, I decided to send him. I have nothing certain to write to my lord concerning him. Therefore I have brought him out before you, and especially before you, King Agrippa, so that after the examination has taken place I may have something to write. For it seems to me unreasonable to send a prisoner and not to specify the charges against him."

Now that is the setting for Paul's very eloquent plea. It is commonly called the "defense" of Paul before Agrippa. I totally disagree that Paul is defending himself before Agrippa. I want you to see the scene, and I hope you'll agree with me that he is not defending himself at all!

As I mentioned before, when Paul was converted, the Lord Jesus had said,

"He is a chosen vessel of Mine to bear My name before Gentiles, kings, and the children of Israel."
(Acts 9:15)

Paul went through his entire ministry without the opportunity to appear before kings. But when he was arrested and imprisoned he at last stood before kings. He eventually went to Rome, and it is believed that

there he actually appeared before the great Nero, the
mad emperor of the Roman Empire.

This man Paul is not defending himself before
Agrippa. What he is actually doing is *witnessing* to
Agrippa. Paul is not on trial here. He has already
appealed to Caesar, and being a Roman citizen, that
appeal puts him beyond the jurisdiction of this court.
However, you can see that Festus is on the spot. He has
heard the accusations against Paul, but he knows that
those charges won't stick. He says, "I've got to have
something to present to Caesar before sending this man
halfway across the world. I want him to appear before
you, Agrippa. Maybe you could help me form the
charges against him." So who is on the spot, Paul or
Festus? I say that Festus is on trial and not Paul at all.

Then consider Agrippa. You will finally hear Paul the
apostle say to him,

**"I would to God that not only you, but also
all who hear me today, might become both
almost and altogether such as I am, except
for these chains."**
(Acts 26:29)

Although Paul stood there in chains, we now have the
perspective of nearly two thousand years to look back
on that scene and determine who was in chains and who
was free. Paul the apostle was the man who was free.
He knew what true freedom was in Christ. And there
sits Agrippa, bound by the chains of lust, the chains of
alcoholism, the chains of immorality—a sinner if there
ever was one. Who is the prisoner? Who is free? You

have a twentieth-century vantage point to look back and form your own judgment.

Now I want to come back to Acts 25:23 and pick up the details:

So the next day, when Agrippa and Bernice had come with great pomp, and had entered the auditorium with the commanders and the prominent men of the city, at Festus' command Paul was brought in.

It is an entirely pagan scene. All the formality, all the pageantry and parade which belong to a great nation, Rome displayed that day.

There is the blowing of the trumpet, the rolling of the drum, the band playing "Hail to the Chief!" and here the dignitaries come marching in. With all the purple, with all the formality, with the bowing servants, King Agrippa and his queen take their place, and Festus takes his place. When everything is in order, they hear the clank of chains coming down the hallway, and there steps in this little man. Voltaire called him "that little ugly Jew." I disagree with him. I think he's one of the loveliest men—perhaps not attractive physically, but when this man presented Jesus Christ, may I say to you, *all* men listened to him. And as he steps into this pagan scene, all become silent. He is not defending himself. He is *witnessing* for Jesus Christ before kings, if you please.

Before I became a Christian, at least before I was sure I was a child of God, I fooled around with a little theater. There's nothing quite as miserable as that! I was in it for several years, and I memorized many lines. Unfortunately, I could stand here and quote certain passages out of plays for the next two and a half hours. When I was young, I wish somebody had taught me the Word of God. I have memorized very little of it, but I did memorize the twenty-sixth chapter of Acts. I think I could quote it today if I went over it several times. I memorized it back then because it is without doubt considered, even by the world, as one of the most eloquent messages that ever has been given. I'd recommend that young people, instead of memorizing verses here and there, memorize Acts 26. This is a glorious piece of literature. Now let's look at it:

> **Then Agrippa said to Paul, "You are permitted to speak for yourself." So Paul stretched out his hand and answered for himself: "I think myself happy, King Agrippa, because today I shall answer for myself before you concerning all the things of which I am accused by the Jews."**
> (Acts 26:1, 2)

And I can almost hear a sigh of relief in the heart of the apostle Paul, and I'll tell you why. He has been in prison nearly three years, at least two and a half, and this has been a trial that has gone on and on and on and on. He had been passed along by the rulers in Jerusalem to Felix. Felix had passed him to Festus and Festus is now passing him to Agrippa, and they both will pass him on to Rome. Nobody will come to any clear-cut decision concerning him. He is weary. To begin with, they do not quite understand the case. They do not understand the

background. Now Paul heaves a sigh of relief because
he realizes that King Agrippa knows the Jews' religion,
he knows the background, and he will understand what
Paul is saying. So it is with relief that Paul now ad-
dresses this message to Agrippa:

> **"You are expert in all customs and ques-**
> **tions which have to do with the Jews.**
> **Therefore I beg you to hear me patiently."**
> (Acts 26:3)

Now Paul is asking this man to listen to him—not for
defense, but he is going to try to win him to Christ!

It has always been a question among the many ex-
positors of the Word whether Paul actually believed he
could win King Agrippa. I am of the opinion that Paul
the apostle never presented the gospel without realizing
that the Holy Spirit could convert any person. For the
same reason, even in these days, I as a preacher have
that hope also. I recognize that in any service, at any
time, the Spirit of God can convert. By the way, if He
doesn't do it, it won't be done—that's for sure. It has to
be the work of the Holy Spirit, and that is our encouragement to give out the Word of God. I must say that I
believe Paul had the hope that this man Agrippa might
be converted. Paul is not hopeless when he is witnessing
to him, but with anticipation he is attempting to win
this man for Christ.

Now he says to Agrippa, "Listen to me patiently. I
want to tell you my story. I know *you* will understand
me."

"My manner of life from my youth, which was spent from the beginning among my own nation at Jerusalem, all the Jews know."
(Acts 26:4)

May I say to you that it is expressions like this that make me confident Paul was at the crucifixion of Christ. He says, "As far as Jerusalem is concerned, all the Jews know me. And I know them all up there—the high priest, the second in command, all of them. The Pharisees know me because I happen to be one of them." By this we know that Paul had lived in Jerusalem for some time. This young Pharisee, who hated Jesus Christ as no other ever hated Him, later called himself the chief of sinners. That's not academic, that's not forensic—he was the chief of sinners. Jesus Christ never had another enemy like this man, Saul of Tarsus. Do you think that zealous young Pharisee would have stayed at home on the day they crucified Christ? Of course he would not! He was there, and with the others he shot out the lip in derision. He sat down and watched the agony of Jesus as He hung on the cross. That's when religion sank to its lowest level—when the enemies of our Lord sat down and watched Him die. Later on, after that Damascus Road experience, this is the man who could say to the Galatian Christians, "He loved me and gave Himself for me." In other words, "When I was right there hating Him, He was saying, 'Father, forgive them, for they know not what they do,' and I *didn't* know what I was doing. But I know Him now as my Savior and my Lord." To King Agrippa, Paul said, "My manner of life from my youth, which was spent from the beginning among my own nation at Jerusalem, all the Jews know."

After Saul of Tarsus was converted he stayed out of Jerusalem for several years, and when he finally did come up there, the Christians were afraid of him. In effect they said, "We know that fellow. He's just clever enough and brilliant enough to use this as a ruse to come up here and persecute us and try to destroy the church." They just could not believe that Saul was converted—and it did seem impossible.

Now will you notice as he goes on,

"They knew me from the first, if they were willing to testify, that according to the strictest sect of our religion I lived a Pharisee. And now I stand and am judged for the hope of the promise made by God to our fathers."
(Acts 26:5, 6)

In other words, "My life as a Pharisee was known to them, and now I stand and am judged for the hope of the promise made by God to our fathers."

Paul is now going to the very heart of the gospel, which is the resurrection:

"To this promise our twelve tribes, earnestly serving God night and day, hope to attain. For this hope's sake, King Agrippa, I am accused by the Jews."
(Acts 26:7)

Now what is that hope?

"Why should it be thought incredible by you that God raises the dead?"
(Acts 26:8)

That is the issue. The resurrection, not the crucifixion of Christ, was the real issue.

And, friend, yet today that is the real issue. The liberal pastor can preach on the death of Christ, but he cannot preach on the resurrection of Christ. You should hear the sermons that come out on Easter here in Southern California! I indulge my flesh with the Saturday evening paper, seeing how the boys are going to make it through Easter Sunday. They have their problems because there happens to be a Man back from the dead. What are they going to do with Him? Some time ago one preacher here on Wilshire Boulevard listed as his sermon: "Easter is the Time of Flowers." Oh, my friend, Easter is not the time for scattering daisies. Easter is the time that Jesus Christ came back from the dead! In fact, every Sunday for the early church was a celebration of the resurrection. Paul certainly makes a point of it. He himself has *seen* Him alive!

Note this again, "Why should it be thought incredible by you that God raises the dead?" He's asking Agrippa, befuddled with liquor and with sin, to do a little thinking. In other words, "Is it incredible to you that God should raise the dead?"

"Indeed, I myself thought I must do many things contrary to the name of Jesus of Nazareth. This I also did in Jerusalem, and many of the saints I shut up in prison, hav-

ing received authority from the chief priests; and when they were put to death, I cast my vote against them. And I punished them often in every synagogue and compelled them to blaspheme; and being exceedingly enraged against them, I persecuted them even to foreign cities. While thus occupied, as I journeyed to Damascus with authority and commission from the chief priests, at midday, O king, along the road I saw a light from heaven, brighter than the sun, shining around me and those who journeyed with me. And when we all had fallen to the ground, I heard a voice speaking to me saying in the Hebrew language. . . ."
(Acts 26:9–14a)

That was his native tongue. Although he had the gift of tongues—that is, he could speak in the languages of the tribes he evangelized—when the Lord spoke to him, it was in Hebrew, his native tongue.

"'Saul, Saul, why are you persecuting Me? It is hard for you to kick against the goads.' So I said, 'Who are You, Lord?'"
(Acts 26:14b–15a)

Again I'll have to advance my own opinion. I believe that Paul the apostle was the most brilliant man who has ever walked this earth. Only a man with a giant intellect could have written the Book of Romans. But Paul, brilliant though he was, did not know the answer to the most important question, "Who are You, Lord?" He did not know the Lord Jesus Christ. "And He said, 'I am Jesus, whom you are persecuting.'" You see, the minute you touch one of God's children, one of His born-again ones, you hurt Him.

> **"'I am Jesus, whom you are persecuting. But rise and stand on your feet; for I have appeared to you for this purpose, to make you a minister and a witness both of the things which you have seen and of the things which I will yet reveal to you. I will deliver you from the Jewish people, as well as from the Gentiles, to whom I now send you, to open their eyes, in order to turn them from darkness to light, and from the power of Satan to God.'"**
> (Acts 26:15*b*–18*a*)

All false religions are satanic. The Lord Jesus says that He is sending Paul to the Gentiles to turn them from the power of Satan to God,

> **"'. . . That they may receive forgiveness of sins and an inheritance among those who are sanctified by faith in Me.'"**
> (Acts 26:18*b*)

Now listen to Paul—he is going after Agrippa's soul. He is asking him to make a decision. For Agrippa it is his hour of decision:

> **"Therefore, King Agrippa, I was not disobe-**

dient to the heavenly vision, but declared
first to those in Damascus and in Jerusalem, and throughout all the region of
Judea, and then to the Gentiles, that they
should repent, turn to God, and do works
befitting repentance. For these reasons the
Jews seized me in the temple and tried to
kill me. Therefore, having obtained help
from God, to this day I stand, witnessing
both to small and great, saying no other
things than those which the prophets and
Moses said would come—that the Christ
would suffer."
(Acts 26:19–23*a*)

Oh, he's going to give him the gospel!

"That the Christ would suffer, that He
would be the first to rise from the dead, and
would proclaim light to the Jewish people
and to the Gentiles." Now as he thus made
his defense, Festus said with a loud voice,
"Paul, you are beside yourself! Much learning is driving you mad!"
(Acts 26:23, 24)

This fellow Festus who is sitting there probably doesn't
realize what he's saying. He is listening in order to be
able to get a charge to send to Rome, and he hadn't heard
a thing to help him. The prisoner is *not* defending
himself, he is presenting Christ, and this thing is beyond Festus. He bursts out, "Much learning is driving
you mad!" That Paul was a brilliant man was obvious

to anyone. In other words, Festus cried out, "This learning of yours must be driving you to fanaticism!" I tell
you, he's under conviction! Paul addressed him respect-
fully,

> **But he said, "I am not mad, most noble
> Festus, but speak the words of truth and
> reason. For the king, before whom I also
> speak freely, knows these things; for I am
> convinced that none of these things es-
> capes his attention, since this thing was not
> done in a corner."**
> (Acts 26:25, 26)

Some folk even now are under the impression that
when Jesus Christ died on the cross and was raised
from the dead on the third day it was some sort of
secret known only to a small group. But notice that
Festus, the governor, knew all about it, and Agrippa
the king knew all about it. It was common knowledge
in that day, my beloved. These were historical facts
that were well known. Festus could have immediately
interrupted, "Wait a minute, Paul, you're talking
about something I never heard about before." He
didn't say that because Paul's reference to Jesus'
suffering, death, and resurrection was common
knowledge of that day. They either believed it or
didn't believe it, but they had heard it.

Let me give you a parallel. It was as well known as
the President's visit to Southern California. I didn't see
him, but I believe he was out here. It was a well-known
fact. A hundred years from today some skeptic may

come along and say, "I don't believe that he was ever in Southern California." Well, if I am still around (and I won't be) I wouldn't waste my time arguing with that fellow. I would just say, "You are stupid, brother. I just happen to know that he was here."

"Did you see him there?"

"No, I didn't see him, but it was common knowledge at that time. Everybody knew he was here."

Similarly, the historical facts that constitute our gospel were common knowledge in Christ's day. That is something for us to take into consideration in these days in which many historical facts are being scoffed at or denied by ignorant people. Paul said, "This thing was not done in a corner." It was not denied in that day. There were some strange explanations for it, but the fact that He died and was out of the tomb on the third day was well known and was the fact upon which Paul was resting his argument.

Then Paul goes back after Agrippa—he is the one Paul is after now. He had already appeared before this man Festus, you see.

He asks Agrippa the question point-blank: "King Agrippa, do you believe the prophets?" The interesting thing is that Agrippa, although he was not a proselyte, did believe the Old Testament prophets.

". . . I know that you do believe."
(Acts 26:27)

Paul knew him, and Paul knew his background.

Then Agrippa said to Paul, "You almost persuade me to become a Christian."
(Acts 26:28)

I know the explanations and the translations that are sometimes made of this. For example, it is explained like this: "You'll have to do something more than this to make me a Christian." Friend, I don't believe it means that. I think the translation of our King James Version is accurate at this point. Probably what Agrippa meant was just simply this: "What you are presenting to me is factual, and what you are presenting to me is very convincing. You *almost* make me a Christian—but not quite." Obviously, Paul is not defending himself. He is trying to win Agrippa to Christ. He is *witnessing* to him. He is on the witness stand and not in the prisoner's box, in spite of the fact he is in chains. Paul is asking Agrippa for a decision, and Agrippa knows he is asking for a decision. "Agrippa, do you believe the prophets?" The old boy wouldn't answer. So Paul added, "I know you believe." In other words, "You don't have to answer that; I know you believe the prophets." And then Agrippa just burst out, "Almost, Paul, you persuade me to become a Christian!" The response now of Paul is, in my opinion, conclusive evidence of his motive throughout:

"I would to God that not only you, but also all who hear me today, might become both almost and altogether such as I am, except for these chains."
(Acts 26:29)

And Paul in his gracious manner—there he stands shackled, irons on his feet and chains on his hands—as he holds up those chains, says, "I wish that all of you here were like I am, a Christian, except for the chains." He is expressing his longing for them to have a personal relationship with Christ, but he wouldn't wish chains on any of them.

Again I say, after nearly two thousand years have gone by, we look back and realize that Paul was the one man there who was free. "If the Son of God makes you free, you shall be free indeed." King Agrippa and the other people in that august assembly were bound by sin, bound by politics, bound by the things that still bind men today and hold them in fetters and keep them from coming out for Christ. "You almost persuade me to become a Christian." King Agrippa couldn't decide. Indecision, irresolution, vacillation kept him from eternal life.

Into this universe and why not knowing,
Now whence, like water willy-nilly flowing;
And out of it as wind along the waste,
I know not whither, willy-nilly blowing.
                                    —Author Unknown

That's the way some people are. They go through life, unable to come to a decision. My friend, God made you with a free will, and you *have* to make a decision. You are in the arena of life at this moment. You won't be here long, and while you are here, God requires a decision. You decide whether you are going to heaven or to hell. Agrippa made his decision there that day, and

Paul had given him the opportunity. Oh, the danger of being indecisive, of being *almost*!

Hamlet, prince of Denmark—this was the tragedy of that young prince's life: He could never come to a decision. He could never have come to the point of execution. Finally, when he was even contemplating suicide,

> *To be, or not to be: that is the question:*
> *Whether 'tis nobler in the mind to suffer*
> *The slings and arrows of outrageous fortune,*
> *Or to take arms against a sea of troubles*
> *And by opposing end them?*
>
> *Hamlet*, Act III

Is that what he's going to do? No, he can't commit suicide and he can't live. Oh, the people who can't make a decision in this life. My beloved, may I say to you that God asks you to make a decision.

Remember the two thieves on the cross? A lady who attended my church handed me this poem one day, saying that she had written it after hearing my message about the two thieves who were crucified with Christ:

Two Men

> *As close one as the other to the Savior,*
> *The two condemned to share with Him His hill.*
> *As guilty both, as bitter their reviling,*
> *With nothing left to either but his will.*
> *As far from hope those two, as near to mercy,*
> *Outstretched to both the loving arms of Christ;*

As close, yet one was lost by his own choosing,
And one that very day in Paradise.

—Rosa Ritterhoff

Yes, you have to make a decision, and you don't have to be a king to do it. God says that every one of us has to come to the place where we decide concerning Jesus Christ.

— 11 —

CORNELIUS

Why Good Men Are Not Saved

There is a drug which has become a menace and a danger to mankind, especially to young people. It produces delusions of grandeur. It gives a feeling of exaltation. You can take a trip into a make-believe land out in the wild blue yonder, if you please. This is the experience of a young man in Los Angeles: He was a student who turned on with this drug to expand his outlook on life. As often happens, the drug gave him an overpowering sense of omnipotence. He strode directly in front of a fast-approaching car and raised his hands in the obvious belief that he could *will* the speeding vehicle to an instantaneous halt. He was wrong. He died. This drug is LSD.

May I say to you that there is also a spiritual LSD. It is a drug that is as old as the human race. There is nothing whatever new about it. It is likewise a menace and a danger to the human family. The effect on the personality is the same, however. It gives folk the delusion that a human being is good enough to stand in God's presence on his own, that he can stand naked there, and God must accept him as he is and take him on his own terms—believing, of course, that man is not actually a sinner.

This spiritual LSD has been given out to the human family since the days of Cain who attempted to impress God by bringing a little offering which represented his own little efforts and his own character. He thought that he would be acceptable to Almighty God. But he was not. Today that same error is being preached—that we are accepted on the basis of our own character and our own little good works. May I say, that is a sugarcoated pill. It is a spiritual delusion. The enemy has been deceiving us. The Word of God is clear: "All have sinned and fall short of the glory of God" (Romans 3:23).

However, when a so-called good man will come God's way, recognizing his need and facing the reality of this life and the life to come, God will save him. The man we are going to look at now did exactly that. His name was Cornelius. He was one of the first gentile converts to Christ after Pentecost. On the day of Pentecost as recorded in Acts 2, as far as we can tell, all believers were Israelites. There was not a Gentile in the lot. The early church was made up strictly of those who belonged to the nation of Israel. It was not until about eight years later in the home of Cornelius, where a group of Gentiles had come together, that there took place what is called—and rightly so—the gentile Pentecost.

Now in the tenth chapter of the Book of Acts, you have God's record of this great transition period from law to grace. It is how God brought men over the high mountain pass of the cross between the valley of law and the valley of grace. God is outlining His program and stating His purpose for this age. He has recorded in the Book of Acts three remarkable conversions, chosen because they represent the entire spectrum of the human family. These are the three ethnological divisions we read about in Genesis 10: the conversion of the Ethiopian eunuch (Acts 8), who was a descendant of Ham; the conversion of Saul of Tarsus (Acts 9), a descendant of Shem; and the conversion of the Roman centurion Cornelius (Acts 10), a descendant of Japheth.

Now I want you to meet this man. He's a most unusual fellow. He is a man worth knowing long before he is converted. Will you notice his name:

There was a certain man in Caesarea called Cornelius, a centurion of what was called the Italian Regiment.
(Acts 10:1)

The name *Cornelius* may not mean very much to us, but it identifies him with either of the two leading families of Rome, two of the oldest families. One was a patrician family and the other was a family of freed slaves who had become outstanding. They included men like Scipio, the Roman general who defeated Hannibal in northern Africa, and Sulla, who as dictator took the power away from the people and gave it to the Senate. This man Cornelius had a remarkable background. He had character. He had good parents and a good genealogy, if you please.

His vocation was that of a soldier. And a Roman soldier was rough and tough and often very brutal. They were probably the best-disciplined soldiers the world has ever seen. Now this man was not only a soldier, he was a centurion. That means he was an officer. He belonged to the brass. He had a prominent position.

In the Roman army, the large group was the *legion*. Its size varied from 4,000 to 6,000 men, depending on the time of Roman history. The *generals* were chosen by the emperor, and under them were *tribunes*. But the most important leaders were sixty noncommissioned officers called *centurions,* each of whom led a *century,* a unit made up of one hundred men. They were the ones deployed over the entire Roman Empire. They kept law and order in that vast empire. There were actually thirty-two of these centuries that were unusual, and these particular troops were called the Italian Regiments. That means they were special. They were volunteers from Rome who were stationed in this strategic place, Caesarea, to keep order and to put down riots. Among the Jews at this time there was a great deal of disorder, and it was on the Italian Regiments that Rome rested for peace and for law and order.

Cornelius, this centurion with an Italian Regiment, was in Caesarea to keep order. Caesarea, not Jerusalem, was really the capital of Judea at this time. Pontius Pilate, the Roman governor of Judea, went to Jerusalem only at the time of Jewish feast days to ensure law and order, and I suppose that often Cornelius went along with him. He was part of that vast police force of his day. He believed in discipline, he believed in law and order, and he was brought up in that philosophy in Rome. Rome owed a great deal to this man and those who were like him. For Cornelius, the military was his vocation.

As to his spirituality, he was a religious man. We are told here that he was devout:

A devout man and one who feared God with all his household, who gave alms generously to the people, and prayed to God always.
(Acts 10:2)

Candidly, I cannot convey to you the meaning of the Greek word *eusebes*, translated *devout* in English. We have no English word for it at all. It is becoming increasingly difficult to express ourselves accurately in English. I wonder if you recognize that. Take the word *economy* for example. When you say that you want the economy size in toothpaste, it's the large size; but in automobiles, it's the small size. So what *is* the economy size? You see, we have trouble today with the English language, and the word *devout* is difficult to define. Well, the word means worship rightly directed. Among the Romans and Greeks, this is the definition that one of them gave: "a recognition of dependence upon the gods." Then let me bring forth this definition which is the best I can do: Cornelius was a man of deep devotion and a man of real conviction. That is Cornelius, as far as religion is concerned.

He was an outstanding man. We are told he feared God. What an eye-opener that is. It means that when he came into the land of Israel, he was a pagan who worshiped the Roman gods. Then he found out about the living and the true God and learned to fear Him. As a Gentile he evidently was a proselyte of Judaism, but not in the strict sense of the term. The Jews of that day had two classifications: First were the *proselytes of righteousness* who went all the way and were circumcised. The others were called the *proselytes of the gate.* They never got into the temple area except into the court of the Gentiles. Apparently that would define Cornelius. He never went all the way. He was just one of those religious men who hears about the living and the true God and fears Him. A remarkable man.

Then we are told he "gave alms generously." Israel laid great stress upon the giving of alms. You will find our Lord mentioned that in the Sermon on the Mount. He also said to the rich young ruler who came to Him, "Sell all that you have and distribute to the poor." You see, the giving of alms occupied a very prominent place, and Cornelius "gave alms generously to the people," which means the Jewish people. He felt indebted to them because of the fact he had come to a knowledge of the living and true God.

It is quite interesting that even today, because of their background in the giving of alms, many of our charitable foundations have been founded by Jews. They have this background and they put the church to shame in what they are giving to the little nation of Israel today. They have been brought up that way. Cornelius was a Gentile who caught on and gave much alms. He was an outstanding man.

Then we are told that he prayed to God. The word for

prayer here is an unusual word. It means that he went with petitions, he brought his needs to God. I do not know this, but I suggest to you that this man went to God and said, "O God, I want more knowledge of spiritual things, I need more light." And God heard, and God answered his prayer.

Not only that, he was a man who had influence and, oh, how believers need that today. I wonder if you have noted the extent of his influence here. It says, "A devout man and one who feared God with all his household." His household followed him. And not only that, but we read:

And when the angel who spoke to him had departed, Cornelius called two of his household servants and a devout soldier from among those who waited on him continually. So when he had explained all these things to them, he sent them to Joppa. (Acts 10:7, 8)

This man even had influence among the soldiers that were under him. He was a devout man and that, by the way, is quite a remarkable thing to be said about a man in his position.

As you can see, Cornelius was a good man. He had all the outward features of a Christian and he had them to the highest degree. He was a man who would pass as a Christian today in most of our churches. A zealous personal worker would pass this man by, assuming he was a Christian, in order to get down to a man on skid row to talk to him. But Cornelius was not saved. This man had a great need. May I say to you that this is a man who is an example of one who lived up to the light he had.

I want to call your attention to two verses that I must confess—and I hope this is a secret between us—I do not know what they mean. John 1:9 says, "That was the true Light which gives light to every man coming into the world." This speaks of Christ and the fact that He lights every person who comes into the world. In other words, there is a light that the heathen have, there is a light that every person has who is born into this world. Cornelius lived up to the light he had. I say to you that he is remarkable. The other verse is Romans 1:18, "For the wrath of God is revealed from heaven against all ungodliness and unrighteousness of men [that which is subjective, that which is in the heart, and that which expresses itself], who suppress the truth in unrighteousness." This, I think, means simply that people did not live up to the light that was given them.

Now Cornelius is God's answer to the oft-repeated question: What about the poor pagan or the good heathen who wants to know God and has never had a chance? Is he lost? The answer is, any man on the topside of this earth who will live up to the light he has, God will give him more light always. *Always.* There is only one catch in this type of question. It is a most unlikely supposition. There were no good heathen in Caesarea in the first century and there are no good heathen in America in the present century. The Word of God says, "There is none righteous, no, not one" (Romans 3:10). You may not agree, but you will have to take God's Word for it. Any missionary will tell you that out on the field the heathen are not begging for the gospel. It sometimes takes years and years of witnessing before the Spirit of God will open the hearts of those people. We make a supposition which has no substance in reality: that mankind is looking and longing for the gospel.

Cornelius is a man who lived up to the light he had, and God will move in his behalf. But there is a big problem here. How could God get the gospel to Cornelius? And I submit to you that there were insurmountable barriers. For the first eight years, the church was exclusively Hebrew. When Paul wrote to the Romans he said,

For I am not ashamed of the gospel of Christ, for it is the power of God to salvation for everyone who believes, for the Jew first and also for the Greek.
(Romans 1:16)

"For the Jew first" was not referring to priority. He was talking about chronology, and chronologically the Jew had the gospel first. "To the Jew first and then also to the Gentile." When the gospel finally broke over even into Samaria (see Acts 8:14–25), the mother church in Jerusalem was surprised, but those new believers did not recognize the hand of God in it.

Now the question is, how can the door of the gospel be thrown open to Gentiles? You can be sure of one thing: At that time the church had had no great evangelistic conference to see about getting the gospel to the Gentiles. In fact, they weren't even concerned and had no program at all.

However, at the very moment God was dealing with Cornelius He was also training Paul the apostle yonder in the desert to be a witness to the Gentiles, to be His missionary to the Gentiles. So while Paul was receiving his B.D. (back side of the desert) degree, God sent Simon Peter to the home of Cornelius to open the door to the Gentiles. And I want to say to you that He picked probably the most prejudiced of His apostles. I am almost inclined to call Peter a bigot at this time. This man did not want to go to the Gentiles, and frankly he is the last man I would have picked. He had no qualifications for it whatever, and besides that, he had a barrier that was tremendous.

But the Spirit of God began to move. Recorded here is a detailed and complicated system He worked in order to get this man Simon Peter into the home of Cornelius so that Cornelius and the other Gentiles might hear the gospel. It is obvious that the Holy Spirit is entirely in charge of this. Oh, how we need to learn this. If there is going to be a conversion, the Spirit of God must be in charge. The only genuine work that can possibly be done is work directed by the Holy Spirit. I want you to notice how He moves. This man Cornelius saw a vision, evidently about the ninth hour of the day, which was in the afternoon, the time of the evening sacrifice. This information simply tells us he was not asleep, it is not a vision given in a dream at night:

About the ninth hour of the day he saw clearly in a vision an angel of God coming in and saying to him, "Cornelius!" And when he observed him, he was afraid, and

said, "What is it, lord?" So he said to him, "Your prayers and your alms have come up for a memorial before God."
(Acts 10:3, 4)

I want to say that in and of itself this is remarkable. This man did not have a dream that God had heard his prayers. Let me repeat this: His prayers and his alms did not save this good man. If any man who is on record could have been saved by his works, it would have been Cornelius. If there is any man who could have been saved by religion, it was Saul of Tarsus. But neither one of them was saved by religion or by good works. However, Cornelius's prayers and his alms had come up for a memorial before God, and God was going to see that he got more light.

Notice, the Spirit of God directs Cornelius:

"Now send men to Joppa, and send for Simon whose surname is Peter. He is lodging with Simon, a tanner, whose house is by the sea. He will tell you what you must do."
(Acts 10:5, 6)

That's all Cornelius was told to do. Joppa is only a few miles down the coast from Caesarea. We made that trip, and I don't recall exactly how far it is, but I remember we ate lunch in Caesarea, and I am confident that by two in the afternoon we were in Tel Aviv which is right next to Joppa. It is not very far. But now he is instructed to send down to Joppa to get this man Simon Peter.

At that same moment, the Spirit of God was preparing another man who was to be the human instrument, and believe me, He *had* to prepare Peter. If these messengers had knocked on the door and said, "Would you come up with us to Cornelius the centurion?" they would have found the door slammed in their faces. Simon Peter would not have gone. He would have been very careful to say, "I'm no missionary to Gentiles, that's not my calling. I am not even about to go." And he would not have gone.

Now will you notice:

> **The next day, as they went on their journey and drew near the city, Peter went up on the housetop to pray, about the sixth hour. Then he became very hungry and wanted to eat; but while they made ready, he fell into a trance and saw heaven opened and an object like a great sheet bound at the four corners, descending to him and let down to the earth. In it were all kinds of four-footed animals of the earth, wild beasts, creeping things, and birds of the air.**
> (Acts 10:9–12)

I remember the pictures they used to give me in Sunday school of those animals, and I want to tell you it was quite a zoo! But I am sure of one animal being there and that would have been a pig, and I am confident he was squealing.

> **And a voice came to him, "Rise, Peter; kill and eat."**
> (Acts 10:13)

Peter, who is just a bundle of contradictions, said, "Not so, Lord!" Well now, how can you call Him Lord and at the same time say no to Him? That's inconsistency of the worst sort. And yet this man was emphatic. In other words, "I am not even about to eat." And he has good reason. You find here a man who is saved by the grace of God, used of God on the day of Pentecost, and he can still say, "I've never eaten anything unclean." I say to you he is prejudiced. Don't criticize him, though, because under grace if you don't want to eat, you don't have to—just don't try to put everybody else under your little rules and regulations. The thing is, he was able to say, "Honestly, Lord, I've never eaten anything unclean." The second time and the third time Peter is told the same thing, and he wonders what it all means. In Joppa he doesn't know the reason, but he is going to find out in Caesarea.

There is a knock at the door and a summons:

Now while Peter wondered within himself what this vision which he had seen meant, behold, the men who had been sent from Cornelius had made inquiry for Simon's house, and stood before the gate. And they called and asked whether Simon, whose surname was Peter, was lodging there. While Peter thought about the vision, the Spirit said to him, "Behold, three men are seeking you. Arise therefore, go down and go with them, doubting nothing; for I have sent them." Then Peter went down to the men who had been sent to him from Cornelius, and said, "Yes, I am he whom you seek. For what reason have you come?" And

> **they said, "Cornelius the centurion, a just man, one who fears God and has a good reputation among all the nation of the Jews, was divinely instructed by a holy angel to summon you to his house, and to hear words from you."**
> (Acts 10:17–22)

He has been told to go with these men without questioning it. So they spend the night, and the next day Peter goes with them. If you ever saw a reluctant preacher, this was one. He said, "You mean to tell me that I'm to go to the home of Cornelius, a Gentile?" Well, that's exactly where he is going. And there in Caesarea, he got his eyes opened:

> **And the following day they entered Caesarea. Now Cornelius was waiting for them, and had called together his relatives and close friends.**
> (Acts 10:24)

A remarkable man, isn't he? He wants his family and friends to hear also.

Peter stepped into that house—what a step that was! It was the first time he had ever been in the home of a Gentile, and he was still baffled at God's command to go there.

> **As Peter was coming in, Cornelius met him and fell down at his feet and worshiped him.**
> (Acts 10:25)

I want you to note what Simon Peter said when this happened. In our day there are those who claim to be following in the apostolic succession and expect folk to bow to them and even kiss their big toe. But listen to Simon Peter:

> **But Peter lifted him up, saying, "Stand up; I myself am also a man."**
> (Acts 10:26)

Notice, he reached down and pulled him to his feet, "Stand up! I myself am also a man." I like the way he did that. This man Cornelius was still a pagan, a heathen, and as a Roman he worshiped heathen gods and bowed down to the priests of those gods. Remember he had been instructed by an angel to send for Simon Peter, so he concluded that this man must be really important. Cornelius was doing something that a Roman would do. In substance, Peter says, "First of all, let's get this straight. You don't fall down before me. I'm a man, that's all I am, just a man."

Well, next, Simon Peter practically insults Cornelius:

> **And as he talked with him, he went in and found many who had come together. Then he said to them, "You know how unlawful it is for a Jewish man to keep company with or go to one of another nation. But God has shown me that I should not call any man common or unclean."**
> (Acts 10:27, 28)

He begins by breaking the first rule of homiletics, which is never to start a sermon with an apology. Poor Simon Peter never had the opportunity of going to one of our modern seminaries. If he had, he would not have opened with an apology. Well, he does it. Then he practically insulted Cornelius. He said, "I always believed that I was not to go into a place where it's unclean, but the Spirit of God told me to come in here." What is he saying? "I consider this place unclean." Now you wouldn't go into a person's home and tell him he has a dirty house! Simon Peter did.

> **Then Peter opened his mouth and said: "In truth I perceive that God shows no partiality. But in every nation whoever fears Him and works righteousness is accepted by Him."**
> (Acts 10:34, 35)

And I must add this, goodness *does* count in the high court of heaven. For example, God did not choose Mary to become the mother of Jesus accidentally. Goodness is important in the high court of heaven. But again let us be very clear, it is not salvation! Your goodness, the prophet says, is like a hot wind in summer.

So, this man Cornelius had his prayers heard, and he had lived up to the light he had. Peter said, "Well, I don't know anything to do but just preach the gospel to you." So he begins, as all of the messages begin in the Book of Acts, with the Lord Jesus Christ. Then he comes to the gospel. Listen to him in verses 39 and 40:

"And we are witnesses of all things which He did both in the land of the Jews and in Jerusalem, whom they killed by hanging on a tree. Him God raised up on the third day, and showed Him openly."

This is the gospel, the good news: "That Christ died for our sins according to the Scriptures, and that He was buried, and that He rose again the third day according to the Scriptures" (1 Corinthians 15:3, 4). These are the facts of the gospel, and it is to believe and receive them that saves a man. Cornelius, as all others, needed the remission of his sins.

Listen to Peter again:

"And He commanded us to preach to the people [I think he emphasized that *people* means Jewish people]**, and to testify that it is He who was ordained by God to be Judge of the living and the dead. To Him all the prophets witness that, through His name, whoever believes in Him will receive remission of sins."**
(Acts 10:42, 43)

Every person needs remission of sins. It doesn't make any difference whether he is on skid row or in Beverly Hills. It doesn't make any difference whether he is in jail today or he is sitting in a liberal church or in the most evangelical church—he needs remission of sins. My friend, you and I do not need all of this external application of religious cosmetics, we need to have remission of our sins!

A few years later, Paul, a missionary to the Gentiles, gave in Ephesians 2:11 this description which
fits the condition of this man Cornelius with all of his
goodness:

> **Therefore remember that you, once Gen-
> tiles in the flesh—who are called Uncircum-
> cision by what is called the Circumcision
> made in the flesh by hands—**

Now here is their condition, your condition, and mine,
as Gentiles:

> **That at that time you were without Christ,
> being aliens from the commonwealth of Is-
> rael and strangers from the covenants of
> promise, having no hope and without God
> in the world. But now in Christ Jesus you
> who once were far off have been brought
> near by the blood of Christ.**
> (Ephesians 2:12, 13)

That is the Gentile. Again will you notice what Paul
says in Colossians 1:20–22:

> **And by Him to reconcile all things to Him-
> self, by Him, whether things on earth or
> things in heaven, having made peace
> through the blood of His cross. And you,
> who once were alienated and enemies in
> your mind by wicked works, yet now He has
> reconciled in the body of His flesh through**

death, to present you holy, and blameless, and above reproach in His sight.

What he is saying is simply this: When Christ died on the cross, God took an attitude toward the entire human family that they are all saveable and God is reconciled to them—it does not make any difference who they are. He saved a man on the cross to show that any man can be saved, and the other thief was not saved to let you know that you don't dare presume on the grace of God.

May I say to you, my beloved, God made it very clear in the first century and it is still clear today that He is reconciled to the whole world. Jesus paid that penalty through the blood of His cross; therefore a righteous God can forgive you. God is not a disagreeable neighbor who is waiting around the corner to pounce on the sinner and to find fault with him. God has His arms outstretched and is saying, "Come, and I will give you redemption rest." God is saying to all mankind today, "I am reconciled to you. Now will you be reconciled to Me?" That is the decision all of us must make—even a good person like Cornelius.

Now notice the momentous event which took place next:

While Peter was still speaking these words, the Holy Spirit fell upon all those who heard the word [and only on those who heard the Word]. **And those of the circumcision who believed were astonished, as many as came with Peter, because the gift of the Holy Spirit had been poured out on the**

**Gentiles also. For they heard them speak
with tongues and magnify God.**
(Acts 10:44–46)

The Jewish Christians would not have believed that God
would save Gentiles if this had not happened. The Gentiles spoke in tongues, that is, in languages they had never
learned. And in these languages they were magnifying
God. The very fact that it duplicated the experience he
and the other apostles had had (as recorded in Acts 2)
convinced Peter. He had to have something to convince
him that God had actually saved these Gentiles.

Later on, Peter was down in Jerusalem for the Council of Jerusalem with Paul and Barnabas, who had been
preaching among the Gentiles with great results. But
there were also some Pharisees who, believe me, in-
sisted that the Gentile had to come through the Mosaic
system, be circumcised, and accept the law. There are
a lot of folk like that today too. These Pharisees followed
Paul wherever he went, saying Gentiles had to be circumcised and keep the laws of Moses in addition to
believing on Jesus. And Paul said, "It's time to get
straight on this." For these men were claiming that back
in Jerusalem all of the other apostles disagreed with the
apostle Paul on this subject. Will you notice Acts 15
verse 1:

**And certain men came down from Judea
and taught the brethren, "Unless you are
circumcised according to the custom of
Moses, you cannot be saved."**

And there are many people today who say there is something to be added to trusting Christ in order to be saved. That was the great issue at this Jerusalem Council. Now many who had been witnessing to the Gentiles stood up and spoke of their experiences, and among them was Simon Peter. What did he say? Well, we read here:

Now the apostles and elders came together to consider this matter. And when there had been much dispute, Peter rose up and said to them: "Men and brethren, you know that a good while ago God chose among us, that by my mouth the Gentiles should hear the word of the gospel and believe. So God, who knows the heart, acknowledged them by giving them the Holy Spirit, just as He did to us, and made no distinction between us and them, purifying their hearts by faith. Now therefore, why do you test God by putting a yoke on the neck of the disciples which neither our fathers nor we were able to bear? But we believe that through the grace of the Lord Jesus Christ we shall be saved in the same manner as they." (Acts 15:6–11)

How gracious it was to express it like that.

Peter had told them about Cornelius, and remember that this was the conversion of a good man. It reveals that a good man cannot be saved by his own goodness. My beloved, God is not saving good people. The reason is there are actually no good people. Oh, some are better than others. The question is not concerning what you have done or what you have joined. The question is simply this: Have you had a transaction with Jesus Christ? When you come as a sinner to Christ and receive Him as Savior, then you will be saved. God saved Cornelius and He will save you.